MW00355582

Real Estate Common Sense

Lisa Spencer

Contributors:

Steven Busch
Curt Howell
Maria Mithani
Niles Spencer
Chris Thompson
Kat White

Copyright © 2020 Lisa Spencer

All rights reserved.

ISBN: 978-1-7354641-0-7

DEDICATION

To Uncle Mike who believed in me. Niles who supported me. My family who motivated me, and all of the clients, colleagues and mentors I met along the way who inspired me.

TABLE OF CONTENTS

FORWARD

A Disney story seems like the perfect place to start, since for the past 15 years I have sold real estate in Florida. Walt Disney succumbed to cancer in 1966. As legend has it, even as he was in his final days, he used the ceiling tiles in his hospital room to detail his vision of an ideal city of the future. You may know it as the Experimental Prototype Community of Tomorrow or EPCOT. At the Grand Opening of EPCOT in 1982 in an interview with Lillian Disney, Walt Disney's wife, a reporter commented: "Isn't it sad that your husband is not here to see this? She replied, if he didn't see this, none of us would be here." Walt Disney's vision was clear to him, and he shared that vision with passion and enthusiasm.

Likewise, success in real estate depends on the vision and drive we bring to the experience. Obtaining a real estate license is only the first baby step in fulfilling a vision that may require the cooperation of an entire community. Perhaps it is the freedom and flexibility of owning our own business that attracts us. Maybe our gaze is fixed on building a real estate empire capable of serving thousands of families each year. Each of us is responsible for determining the "WHY." The pages that follow will attempt to fill in the "HOW."

Disney's daughter, Diane, also at the EPCOT Grand Opening, made a comment that sums it up: "It is beautiful, but without the wonderful people who are part of this, it wouldn't be nearly what it is, it would be empty."

We do not sell houses . . . we build relationships! We are going to talk a lot about how important it is to protect the relationships we build. For most people the purchase of a home will be the largest financial investment of their lifetime, and we are going to be a part of that event. How we serve people and who we meet will make a difference, both in our life and the lives of others.

I was three years into a complicated marriage when I began my real estate career in 1994. My household consisted of my husband, his mother, my two daughters from a previous marriage, and my husband's daughter and her toddler son. My husband also had 3 other children that were in various stages of young adulthood that required assistance with education, housing, or emotional support.

I was frustrated by my office administration job that kept me from my home over ten hours a day. The $30,000 a year I earned did not go far, and the anxiety of daily life ran high. Did I mention that my husband's mother also suffered with dementia? Surely the flexibility offered by a career in real estate might be an answer.

I decided to get a real estate license and join my uncle's real estate office. I was no stranger to the real estate business. My uncle actually started at my father's small boutique brokerage several decades earlier. I knew it would be hard work, but I could set my own schedule and, with some effort, be able to match my $30,000 per year salary.

There is a huge temptation to recount the many stories and experiences that have drifted through the river of my life, but the purpose of this book is to help others. It is designed to be a quick read, but then to be used as a reference book to help you evaluate a brokerage, put together a business plan, and maintain focus in a business crowded with distractions. Once your "Real Estate Common Sense" is developed, I urge you to grow with unique and compelling ways to stay relevant in the ever-changing world of real estate.

One of the hardest things about writing this book, my story, is knowing there is someone who has had success doing something completely different than what will be recommended in the pages that follow. There is also the risk of knowing that choosing a career in real estate is choosing to build a business in, what is arguably, the most dynamic industry in the United States of America. Because it is so dynamic there may not be a very long shelf life for information. Especially as it relates to technology, changes are happening at light speed these days.

"Real Estate Common Sense" is an outline of the essentials for real estate success. Some of it will be my opinions which have been formed after over two decades in the real estate business. Most of it is wisdom acquired through my experiences, and that of other top producing agents. It is only fair to share why my opinion may matter, and how I have so many experiences to relay to you.

Remember, I wanted to replace my $30,000 a year salary. I did that my first year. As it turns out, every year that followed my income increased. This happened because I built relationships and a reputation for being a zealous advocate, knowledgeable guide, and all around pretty fun person who loved helping buyers and sellers.

When I left New Jersey in 2005 to move to Florida my combined business in two states produced ten times more than my first year with a GCI of over $300,000. GCI is "Gross Commission Income" which is the money earned before sharing with the broker and others. We will share much more on that later. In 2007 I made a huge career change. and became a "Productivity Coach" and eventually a managing broker for what would become my company's number one office in Florida.

When I left to launch a personal coaching and consulting company for small businesses, our office had grown to 413 agents which had served over 3000 families in 2018. Like Diane Disney, I feel all of that would be empty without the people I have met.

I am a person of action. It is my hope that you are too. Before going to print, I shared this book with a few trusted friends. One of them, Chris Thompson, reminded me of a Chinese proverb: "Better to have a diamond with a flaw, than a perfect pebble." That quote crystalized what we face when launching our own business. If we wait to be perfect, we will miss the diamonds out there. In order to support you in taking action, there are a few "Diamond Assignments" sprinkled throughout this book. I urge you to dive in and complete them. Hopefully with the help of a broker, mentor or coach.

The possibilities of how to succeed in real estate are endless, and the sea of opportunity can also be distracting and confusing. Our intention is to provide focus and direction. After you have acquired your "Common Sense," you will have the opportunity to explore what additional real estate tools and techniques feel right for you. Jump in with both feet. Get 1% better every day and remember to have fun!

SUPPORTING YOUR EXPERIENCE

Proverbs exist so that we can learn from the wisdom of others. Rather than have a "perfect pebble," go for the "diamonds." The diamonds are the actions we take even if those actions are not yet perfected. As a support to your assignments throughout this book, the website www.RealEstateCommonSense.com was developed.

Please confirm any of the samples and systems with your broker as they are not meant to be comprehensive or to be used for compliance to state or local laws and ordinances.

DIAMOND ASSIGNMENT

When you see the "DIAMOND ASSIGNMENTS," reference the appropriate segment of the website for supporting documents which may be helpful as a template for your personal presentations.

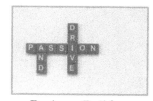
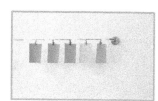

Business Builders	The Buyer Experience	The Seller Experience
Use this for:	Use this for:	Use this for:
✓ Goal Setting ✓ Business Planning ✓ Real Estate Essentials Checklist	✓ Purchase Timeline ✓ Buyer Agreement ✓ Buyer Experience Checklist	✓ 3 Types of Buyer ✓ Knowledgeable Guide ✓ Seller Experience Checklist

YOUR LICENSE & SELECTING A BROKER

Obtain a Real Estate Salesperson License

Every state has different requirements for obtaining a real estate license. "Google" how to get a real estate license in your state, and you will get the information you need, and a multitude of sponsored results leading you to real estate school providers.

If you took a real estate course in college it may meet the classroom requirements, if so, you just have to schedule the state test. In many parts of the country attorneys can conduct real estate transactions as a part of their practice. For the rest of us, we will attend real estate school in person or take a course with specific hourly requirements online.

The cost for licensure varies widely from state to state as well as pre-licensing education requirements, so we won't dedicate much time to that. What needs to be stressed though is that in most states it is a FELONY to conduct real estate without a license. If you are working as an assistant or administrator in a real estate office be sure you are not violating the law by actually doing duties that are restricted to licensed sales people.

Florida has special incentives for veterans. Some companies offer licensure re-imbursement. Remember to ask!

It is actually amazing how inexpensive it is to launch a real estate business in comparison to other small businesses. You should be able to get a license and pay your initial start up fees for less than $3000. These costs can be considerably less depending on the broker you choose. The key is to remember that you are launching a business. You will be an independent contractor under the most common models, so it is best to prepare for a "ramp up" period with some cash reserves.

* This is a great place to mention that all state laws vary and before putting any of the suggestions in this book into practice, you should confirm your state laws and statutes with your broker.

Becoming a Realtor – Or not?

Having a real estate license does not make you a Realtor®.

If you decide to select an office that requires you to be a Realtor® then you will have to join the local, state, and National Association of Realtors®. You will get a complete history and tour of benefits during your orientation.

One difference between real estate sales associates, and Realtors® is an adherence to the "Code of Ethics." This document is updated every year and can be found online at:

https://www.nar.realtor/about-nar/governing-documents/the-code-of-ethics

The National Association of Realtors has an active political action committee, RPAC, that endorses and communicates with political entities to bring forth legislation that continues to support home ownership at the local, state, and federal level.

Your Realtor® dues, MLS (Multiple Listing Service) fees and lockbox key (now an app on your smart phone) in addition to the fees charged by the broker should be budgeted prior to activating your license.

Mentorship and/or Training

In general, your real estate licensing exam taught you that an acre consists of 43,560 square feet, and how to stay out of jail. I have been licensed in two states and neither one of those tests taught me how to have success as a real estate professional.

Without some type of support, you will be experiencing "Baptism by fire" which will benefit neither you nor your customers.

This book is meant to provide some "common sense" tools and a roadmap to help you navigate the twists and turns that are a part of the dynamic world of real estate. It is not meant to replace or diminish the value of a mentor, or comprehensive training provided by a broker.

Feel free to use what we share to "benchmark" the quality of what is being offered to you by the broker you choose.

Selecting a Broker

In most states, you will need to select a broker. With the exception of a few, the state requires new licensees to work under a supervising broker. The requirements for "supervision" vary greatly from state to state. Some states require the broker to review and sign every document that their agents execute for consumers. In other states this "supervision" is much less stringent.

Regardless of the requirements of broker supervision choosing a broker is one of the most important decisions we make when launching a real estate career. Unfortunately, many agents join the brokerage of a friend or fall into a relationship with a broker because their licensing course was held at the brokerage.

In my years of interviewing agents, their questions usually focused on:

- Splits – How will the money I earn be divided?
- Space – Where will I sit when I work?
- Software – How will the technology help me?

Although these are important questions, the following four questions had more of an influence on the success of the agent, and their longevity with our firm:

- Coaching – How important is personal and professional growth?
- Collaboration – Are fellow agents sharing their best practices?
- Culture – Is the office a high energy, positive environment?
- Community – Will my contribution make a difference?

Your relationship with your broker is your first partnership. It is an important relationship and one that should not be entered into lightly. When I started, I took a short cut because I went to work with my favorite uncle, quite possibly my favorite person on earth, so the most important factor of trust was already built in. Make this decision slowly and purposefully and change it quickly if it is a wrong fit. The longer you are in the business the harder it is to change brokerages.

Here are 10 important questions to ask during your broker selection interview:

1. **Is there a mentorship or training program?**
2. **Are the agents Realtors®?** – Is it an important distinction to you? Remember, not all real estate agents are Realtors®.
3. **What marketing collateral is provided by the office?** – Website, signs, buyer and seller presentations, business cards, open house signs or other signage. *A helpful chart is on page 48*
4. **What technology is used by the brokerage?** Is there an e-signature platform and document storage? Is there a CRM – Customer Relationship Management system? Who will help you learn these systems?
5. **How will the broker assist with building your business?** Are leads provided? If so, how are they distributed: round robin, performance, seniority, etc.?
6. **How is the compensation structured?** This varies widely!
7. **What fees are required by the brokerage?** Is there a registration fee, monthly fee, technology fee? Ask about the details. Are there any other fees?
8. **Does the broker compete?** Which means you and your broker may possibly be going on an appointment with the same potential seller. Will you feel comfortable with the broker having access to your database of clients?
9. **What happens if you decide to leave?** In many states all listings belong to the broker. Will the broker let you take your listings with you when you leave? Most brokers require you to close any fully executed contracts with the brokerage. Will there be a penalty if you leave before closing? Will your contract be assigned to someone else to close, which interferes with your relationship with your client, and may require you to pay a hefty referral fee?
10. **How much does the broker love real estate?** Passion and enthusiasm go a long way in this business. Ask about their favorite part of their job – Is it about helping others grow? This is the winning answer!

REAL ESTATE ESSENTIALS

Now that you have taken some time to be mindful about your selection of a broker, we will explore 8 essential skills every real estate salesperson should master. From this point forward in the book, we will also refer to a real estate professional as a Realtor®. After the initial outline we will take a deep dive into each essential skill. We have provided the wide margins to encourage you to add notes and information you gather on how to modify and improve these essentials to accommodate your local laws and protocols.

Too many Realtors® rely on personality and the strength of the relationship with their clients to see them through a transaction. This is a great disservice to the consumer and will make for a frustrating if not, short lived, career. This book and the companion website www.RealEstateCommonSense.com are designed to assist you in developing and improving the essential skills of real estate professionals.

The 8 Essential Skills of Real Estate Success

#1   **Where to Find New Business!**

Depending on the source, statistics show that only 10-15% of Realtors® are still in the business after 5 years.

Success depends on an immediate plan on how to generate new business. There are some companies or real estate teams that will offer to provide "leads." This will come at a price. One that may also stall the ultimate goal of developing "your" real estate business. We will discuss "to TEAM or not to TEAM" on page 22.

If you focus on providing a superior customer experience for your clients, your business will grow exponentially through referrals. The first few years can feel like a roller coaster with the – up - of frantically trying to service your customers at a high level then – down - staring at a phone waiting for it to ring.

Your ability to prospect, lead generate, cold call, host open houses, network or what ever else you want to call the ability to **find new business**, will determine your ability to have an enjoyable healthy real estate career.

Internet lead generation has become a "double edged sword." Some agents have become dependent on internet lead sources. The caution is how quickly the fees and parameters change. The more relationships you personally build, the more control you will have over where your business comes from and how consistent you can be in delivering a great experience.

#2   **Mastering the use of the Multiple Listing Service**

Technology is moving at lightning speed and will have changed since the printing of this book.

The Multiple Listing Service is more than just an exchange of listings. It will often be a valuable resource for you. You will likely find tax data, community information, property history and other data that will help you be a knowledgeable resource for buyers and sellers.

When you are starting out, investing time in really digging deep in to what services are offered by your MLS will be well spent. It may even give you an advantage over the seasoned agents that are too busy to learn "new tricks." Take advantage of the time you have now!

#3   **An Internalized Listing Presentation**

What value are your bringing to sellers? If you are not sure of what it is, you will never convince them.

Does your broker provide a presentation, on how they assist with marketing homes? It is important for you to understand the advantages of your tools, and systems.

I have never gone on a listing appointment where a seller did not want to sell their home for the best price, in the least amount of time, with the least inconvenience. Focus on addressing these three issues within your presentation.

#4   ## An Internalized Buyer Consultation

Not taking time for a buyer consultation is probably the biggest mistake made by new agents. They think they are simply "showing" properties. When in fact, our role is one of the "Calm and Knowledgeable Guide" . . . this has been a mantra of mine for years as a broker, and you will see many versions of this phrase again throughout this book.

"First Time Home Buyers," above all other types of buyers deserve to have the home buying process explained to them with patience and in detail.

A properly internalized and executed "Buyer Consultation" will save you time, and your buyers heartache and frustration.

#5   ## Knowledge of the Local Real Estate Market

Even if you are not a numbers person, you need to have some basic statistics available to support your buyers and sellers in making good decisions.

You will also need to become the "source of the source" for local school information, economic development plans, trending market values, and a host of other information that could impact the value of homes in your area.

The more you study and know about the community and the market, the more valuable you become to buyers and sellers.

#6   ## Transaction Management

One of the reasons being a Realtor® is so interesting is that no two transactions are the same. The conditions of every sale involve the transfer of property, the personality of the buyer and seller, and potentially up to 30 additional service providers that will take the sale to the finish line.

At the center of all of this is you, the Realtor®. Because of the complexity of each individual sale it is difficult to develop and manage a comprehensive checklist or system. Some brokers offer transaction management services, for a fee, to their agents.

#7   **A Business Plan**

Working without a business plan is a critical mistake made by agents. They think they just got a "job" in real estate. However, most Realtors® are independent contractors which means we are a "business!"

Understanding how the money is earned and what expenses are around the corner will keep your doors open. The sooner you can operate from a "Profit and Loss statement," the sooner you will be building a sustainable business.

"Real Time" goal setting and strategies for executing those goals should also be incorporated in your business plan.

#8   **Marketing, Technology, and Social Media**

This is, and always will be, a moving target. Consider this content on the subject an attempt to assist you with an outline of the multi-media tools available to grow your business and serve buyers and sellers.

This book was written as a diversion during the COVID 19 pandemic of 2020. Hopefully the virus has become a distant memory. What will, most definitely, stay with us are some of the innovative solutions agents have maximized to market their listings using technology, social media, and other amazing marketing avenues.

Virtual Staging, Facebook live video premieres, and consultations being done through internet meeting rooms, such as Zoom are just a few of the dramatic changes that were quickly implemented during this time. They most likely will be adopted permanently for their efficiency and ability to increase marketing to a larger buyer pool moving forward.

BONUS – Your Vision

Your unique approach to real estate and life. You will attract who you are. So be fun, kind, and possess a sense of adventure!

ESSENTIAL #1

Where to Find New Business

Where to find new business is the number one real estate essential for a reason! As we cover the sources of business, I am going to name 10. There are many more. As a matter of fact, the list could be endless. In the beginning you should focus on 3. Once those are mastered, add more sources. Finally, you should build and keep, if you don't already have, a fantastic base of previous customers that will support, and advocate for your business.

In my experience, it takes about 5 years to establish a solid referral stream and even then, you will never be able to stop finding new business. You never know when your best referral source will get a real estate license, or when the attorney that has referred his probate clients for years will decide to sell his practice.

There is no particular order or preference to this list. Which one "hits" you as – "Yep, I can do that" - DO THAT!!! The operative word is, "DO," get into action quickly. There are a lot of moving parts in a real estate transaction, and if you wait until you are confident in perfect execution, you will starve.

This is also where we need to talk about time. We cannot manage time. We need to reserve time to accomplish our goals. Most of us do that through "Time Blocking." In order not to slow the pace and purpose of this book, we will not give it more than this paragraph. I work with a proven color coded "reservation" system. It is one of my most widely attended workshops. Agents later return to show me how they implemented the system. It is rarely an accurate representation of how "I" do it. Who cares! If it works to keep them focused and productive, we have accomplished our goal. Whether you "bullet journal," use a google calendar, a checkbook sized paper calendar, figure out a way to schedule time for building, supporting and maintaining your business. The first reservations in your calendar go to you and those you love. Put them on the calendar. Those reservations are sacred. The rest of the time is flexible and available to support your amazing career.

Source #10

"For Sale by Owner" or the infamous F.S.B.O.

*** Please consult your broker regarding your "Do Not Call" policy.
The following suggestions assume and in-person visit.**

From now on think of them as "Talented do it yourselfers, marketing their home on their own."

Some sellers marketing their home on their own have had a bad experience with a Realtor® in the past. Some have watched too much HGTV and think it is about showing their home to the thousands of buyers that are just waiting for a home just like theirs to enter the market. Some are just "testing" the market and have a Realtor® at the ready when they are sure they can't sell it on their own.

Regardless of the reasons, here is where I have had success in working with "Talented do it yourselfers, marketing their home on their own."

Show the home to a potential buyer

One of the reasons I had advocates for my real estate business was my "dog after a bone" determination in finding the right home for the buyers I served. I would ask them WHERE they wanted to live and, after exhausting the available inventory on the MLS, I would visit every FSBO to ask if they would consider paying a commission if I brought them a buyer? Many said yes.

Please do not run with this idea with "fake" buyers. Those who do this are being deceptive and tarnish our reputation. If you don't have an active buyer for a FSBO property you can ask to preview their home, as you like to know all of the available inventory in your area. During your preview you can discuss the possibility of cooperation should you be working with a buyer in the future. This conversation is most fitting if you attend a FSBO open house.

Visiting a "For Sale by Owner" Open House

Visiting the open house of someone marketing their home on their own is a great way to introduce yourself. It was my practice to visit open houses in my market area as a way to increase my knowledge of the local inventory of available homes.

The following is a favorite FSBO conversation:

"There are 3 types of buyer. The ideal buyer, the local buyer, and the investor.

The 'ideal buyer' is moving in from out of the area, and depends on the services provided by local real estate professionals.

They rely on their Realtor® for area information, guided tours, and insight into local economic growth and community development.

These buyers are relocating within a specific time frame and need a home now. They are usually willing to pay market value for a home in order to meet their time constraints. They welcome the guidance of their Realtor® as an essential part of a successful move to a new area.

A change in circumstance or the desire to buy a first home is often the motivation for the 'local buyer.'

These 'locals' know the neighborhoods, and the pace of area real estate sales. They will often wait for just the right house, and can pass on options above fair market value.

Local buyers prefer to work with their Realtor® because they need help with coordinating the sale of a previous home, help with financing options, or guidance as first-time homebuyers. They often have trusted real estate professionals in their circle of friends and family.

The 3rd type of buyer is the investor. Most investors are looking for bargains.

If they are 'flipping' the home, they must be aware of the margins for profit, and usually use a "wholesale" number rather than market value in their calculations."

A new type of investor, the iBuyer, has appeared in recent years. These buyers, investors, use agents or computer algorithms to make offers on homes sight unseen. This is convenient for sellers and when prices are on the rise, this model has some benefit. The iBuyer revolution creates a convenience factor for home sellers that may be worth the reduced retention of equity, but most sellers would rather realize the highest return on their investment.

Explaining to a "For Sale by Owner" that someone marketing their home on their own may find themselves excluded from the "ideal buyer" and have limited exposure to local buyers sometimes provides an opportunity for you to offer your services, that are now more valuable than they realized. Many sellers like to "test" the market, and often turn to the services of a Realtor® when they feel that they have exhausted their own marketing efforts.

In my experience using scare tactics or stressing the failure of other consumers who attempted to sell on their own rarely worked for other Realtors® and was something that didn't feel right for me. Instead, I kept in contact with them and offered assistance. Sharing a trusted mortgage lender's information as a way for them to pre-approve their buyer or helping them understand "next steps" and giving them information for a most valued real estate attorney showcased my ability to connect people with what they need.

Keep in touch with "For Sale by Owners." Many of them eventually list.

DIAMOND ASSIGNMENT

Visit a "For Sale by Owner" listing. The "3 Types of Buyer" conversation is available in pdf form on www.RealEstateCommonSense.com

Source #9

Expired Listings

For Sale by Owners and Expired Listings are the two most common forms of prospecting. Agents that intend to have a big business and a daily lead generation habit will engage in prospecting for "now" business. "For Sale by Owner" and "Expired Listings" are the consumers raising their hands for assistance.

You can jump in with the aggressive cold callers or move to more creative ways to interact with these two sources of business. As mentioned in my approach to "Talented do it yourselfers marketing their home on their own," or FSBO's, I found in-person interaction to be the most productive way to interact.

For the realm of expired listings I looked to the "old expireds" for new business. Once the homeowner gets over the disappointment of their home not selling, and the barrage of cold callers that called immediately upon expiration of their former listing agreement subsides, they are more open to real estate conversations.

6 months after the home expires there is a new market to participate in and new buyers that have entered the buyer pool. You may need to do some research to confirm that they have not re-listed with another Realtor®, but this was a regular source of new business for me.

Regarding For Sale by Owner and Expired listings, approach them in the way that feels right to you. Success exists just past the limits of our comfort zone, so stretch a bit!

IMPORTANT NOTE

Please consult with your broker for a list of local "Do Not Call" numbers as well as consulting the "National Do Not Call Registry." Heavy fines are associated with violating "do not call" restrictions.

Source #8

Professional Advocates

Third-party endorsements are so much better than you advertising the benefits of your services. Start developing your professional advocates immediately, they will be your partners in many transactions.

Start with getting advocates of any kind. Start with your mom. Make the call! "Mom, I just started a career in real estate, and I need to ask you a favor. Will you promise me that if you hear of anyone interested in buying, selling or investing in real estate you will give them my contact information? Better yet, will you ask if it is ok for you to share their information with me."

It sounds silly, and until you feel the stab of someone in your mom's bunko group listing with someone else, you will not understand how you cannot take anything for granted. Help everyone you know understand how to refer business to you.

Then, hold everyone you pay for service accountable to becoming a referral partner. The person who cuts your hair talks to tons of people every week. Patronize local small businesses for as many goods and services as you can. Rather than go to a big box store, are there places where you can shop, and engage in supporting, a small business network that can feed your referral pipeline?

Ribbon cuttings and happy hours cannot take the place of true connections and active participation in the community where you list and sell homes. Be visible in your community as a lead provider. Your success with professional advocates will have a direct correlation to how successful you have been in building the business of others.

DIAMOND ASSIGNMENT
"SHOP LOCAL"

Source #7

Open Houses

Market conditions can impact the level of success you have with hosting open houses. There is also a direct link to the amount of advanced effort you put in to hosting an open house.

Obtain the seller's permission to host an open house. Bring some key items to every open house. Nicely scented disinfecting wipes, paper towels, and a garbage bag especially if you are serving food. The seller should not return to their home and find anything disturbed, missing, or rotting in unattended garbage.

Turn on the lights, play some background music and be prepared to review other homes in the area and how they compare to the home you are holding "open."

It is a great practice to host an open house with another agent for your safety. You could also bring a spouse or friend just for security if you are concerned about how to share the leads. Please be sure to check real estate laws in your area. Some states are quite strict about what can be said by an unlicensed person at an open house. Your spouse is there for security only if they don't have a license.

Confirm that the home has been promoted on internet sites as an open house. This is especially important if you are hosting an open house for another Realtor®. Don't assume that they promoted it, confirm it.

Check with local ordinances regarding directional signs. If they are permitted, load up. Place directional signs from the street with the heaviest traffic and at each turn heading toward your open house.

On open house day, you are "ON!" If you are placing signs, purchasing balloons, or parking your car, people are watching you. Some are watching to see how hard you work to get your listings sold because they are thinking of selling next year, or next week.

If you don't have listings to host as open houses, then ask your broker or a top agent in your office if you can "borrow," meaning host an open house, at another agent's listing.

Source #6

Circle Prospecting

The basic principle of "Circle Prospecting" is to let all of the surrounding homes around a new listing know about the home. There are services that can be purchased that will provide phone numbers. Because of "Do Not Call" phone restrictions many agents use postcards or engage in door knocking campaigns to accomplish this.

I made business card size promotional flyers for my listings and shared at least 20 a week for each of my listings. It sounds like a small number, and once you are carrying a decent listing inventory it can become challenging. Rather than give out a business card with a ridiculous "glamour shot" on it, I shared my active listing cards, which all had my contact information on them. The old "two birds with one stone" idea. If you add layers of marketing beyond the MLS, you fulfill a promise to the seller and create opportunities to grow your business.

UPDATE – Keeping your "Business Card" in an electronic vCard or other electronic format is an acceptable (if not preferred) "GREEN" alternative to the Victorian Era "Calling Card." Again, do what works for you and is well received by the consumers you serve.

DIAMOND ASSIGNMENT

Host an OPEN HOUSE and CIRCLE PROSPECT around the address 2 days prior to the open house. Share a marketing piece and extend the invitation to friends and family.

Source #5

Farming or Target Marketing

The definition of farming when I got my license in 1994 consisted of postcards, newsletters and neighborhood events. Now, facebook groups, meet up gatherings, and other solutions have emerged. The overall idea is regular communication which connects you with real estate to a group of people you haven't met. The hope is that they will make a sort of connection when they have a real estate need.

It is called "farming" because you are planting seeds for the future. You will dramatically increase the results if you use farming to identify a group of people with which you intend to build deeper relationships.

You can set your farm as:

Geographic – A specific neighborhood or geographic area.

Demographic- People who have owned their home 10+ years, absentee owners, or other target audience.

Psychographic – Potential buyers and sellers that share a hobby or interest such as golfers, boaters or equestrians.

At the time of publication, I am still receiving postcards from the top agent in my neighborhood. I know her personally and she would not do it, if it was not producing some results.

Against my advice another agent in our office is still sending recipe postcards, and I overheard her claiming her newest listing came from one of them. So . . . what do I know? Her enthusiasm and authenticity are making it work for her!

Farming illustrates a double-edged sword. An agent that farms an area will never replace a valued and trusted agent. Sadly, many agents neglect consistent communication with their former customers and sphere of influence which makes their clients vulnerable to calling the agent on the most recently "boosted" listing. In the age of "instant gratification" a commitment to farming your own "people" must be a part of your business strategy. Put a system in place to communicate your value as a resource for "all things real estate" to all of the contacts in your phone today. This is your first and most important farm.

Source #4

Networking

The first network that comes to mind is one of the professionally designed networks such as BNI – (Business Network International and their many knock offs) Networks can also be organizations that connect you to the community. The Rotary Club, local Chamber of Commerce, or a charity that you are passionate about would also be considered "networks." It can also be an informal book club, scrapbooking group or the network of parents waiting in the car line after school each day.

Finding the balance between shameless self-promoter and too humble to instill confidence that you can get the job done can be a delicate one. This is why outside of a network that is specifically put together for business purposes, you will be wise to select something in which you have a genuine interest.

My advice would be to find a network that feels "authentic." A community where you feel supported and you feel like you are supporting others through fun activities and events.

Whether your network is formal or informal make it purposeful. Use your network to grow and deepen relationships, and business referrals will become a welcome by-product. If you are the neon "taker" in the group, only there to receive leads, you are wasting your time.

Networking is most productive when it is a regularly scheduled event. Show up and participate with enthusiasm.

DIAMOND ASSIGNMENT

Select a charitable organization or networking group that excites you, and find out how to join. Put the meeting times on your calendar, and commit to attending every event this year.

Source #3

Garage Sales or Online Classifieds

It is surprising how many people do a massive purge of stuff as a first step in the process of moving. Rather than visit these yourself, find a friend or family member that loves garage sales and give them a fancy cardholder loaded with your business cards.

We can contemporize the garage sale method through regular visits to online classifieds on facebook, nextdoor, or craigslist. Again, this will work much better if you have a friend or family member that loves to shop the "vintage" circuit. Just last week my husband purchased a used bicycle through our "nextdoor" community. When he picked up the bike the seller informed him, he was cleaning out the garage because he and his wife were thinking of selling. True story, June 2020.

Source #2

Never eat lunch alone

This is still a personal favorite for me. If you are ever asked to join someone for lunch, say yes! Fellow agents will share their latest challenges or victories and you will learn from their experiences.

The better lunch date comes from your "Sphere of Influence" which will be further defined in detail on the coming pages. Can you budget for lunch at least once a week with someone that you feel could impact your business? Your broker, a top agent in the office, a mortgage lender, an attorney, your cousin that you haven't spoken to for months or years, are just the tip of the iceberg. So many people would benefit from an hour of dedicated time.

Make the lunch about them, be interested in their life and events instead of focusing on an agenda. The law of reciprocation will influence them to ask about you. Wait for it. Be brief and optimistic, you cannot inspire anyone with pessimism. After lunch send a thank you note with a special line validating your conversation, showing you were listening. This is magic in your personal life too!

Source #1

Sphere of Influence

Have you noticed that our 10 sources for new business have been in "countdown" form? I have listed them in the order in which I had success. These were my top 10 and without question and the "Sphere of Influence" is numero uno! Sphere of Influence, or SOI, is widely interpreted and loosely defined to the point of no longer resonating with us. If it ever resonated with us at all?

So, let's take a different approach! Rather than putting ourselves in the center of the universe alone with a golden lasso trying to pull people into our sphere, think of yourself as a gem dropping into a lake of opportunity. You were dropped into that lake on the day you were born, and you are starting your real estate "ring" today. You will need to lean on the relationships formed from birth until today. Family, friends, classmates, associates, and acquaintances will be your foundational relationships. What history are you bringing forward into your new "ring" of opportunity? Are there any relationships we need to repair? Are there relationships we can strengthen for mutual benefit?

Over time your "Sphere of Influence" will grow by your interactions with people you have assisted with real estate transactions. Until you build that database, start with these:

1. **Who, in your world, is vested, interested, and cheering for you?** Your spouse, your parents, and your best friend are your first advocates. Have you enlisted them in the launch of your new business? Each of them will encounter up to 6 people this year that have a real estate need.
2. Your friends and associates may have heard you got a real estate license. These are the connectors in your world. Have you built up enough "credits" with your friends to ask them for help? One of the best ways to enlist them is by being a connector for them. Make a conscious effort to help others with their projects, or charities or new businesses. **How many "connectors" will commit to referring business to you? Ask them.**

3. Now, in my opinion, the 3rd and final group. The people who you recognize and can remember their name, and a point of reference. They are the parents at your children's school. They are someone from your golf club, they are members of any group of people with whom you regularly associate. **Can you shift the reference of these acquaintances?** If you can move them from thinking of you as someone they like and trust in a social arena to someone that they would consider for their real estate needs, you are on your way to cultivating and maintaining a "Sphere of Influence."

Having 10 sources for new business is just a start. If you explore suggestion #2 and take some agents to lunch, ask them to share their best source of business. You will find many of them have developed unique and resourceful ways to keep meeting new people that want to buy, sell or invest in real estate.

DIAMOND ASSIGNMENT

A B C's of finding new business!

Write down the alphabet on a piece of paper:

A – Attorney, Aunt …., Astronaut (just kidding)

…but not really, maybe you know an astronaut?

B – Barber, Banker, Builder

C – Contractor, Cosmetologist, Chiropractor

You get the idea. Now replace the title with names by googling that category. You will have more success, if by writing the title, you thought of someone you already know. Reach out to them today and ask if they know anyone you can help buy, sell or invest in real estate. Be a resource. Offer them something of value. A report, market data, connection to your unique services can all be helpful.

"To TEAM or not to TEAM" That is the question!

One of the most fascinating developments in the past two decades in real estate is the "Team Model." Real estate has always been locally driven. Realtors® are connectors and usually deeply entrenched in their local community. Top agents grew "teams" that permitted them to leverage functions that didn't require people connections like marketing, transaction management and appointment setting.

Real estate agents that focused on listings soon became overwhelmed with leads once the internet multiplied the leads that used to only be driven by postcards and sign calls. Thus the "buyer's agent" model was born. When a newer agent joins a team, as a buyer's agent, they are given instant access to buyer leads. This sounds like a no-brainer, right? Not so fast.

The listing agent, sometimes called a lead agent or rainmaker, will maintain the relationship with the buyer after the sale and most team contracts stipulate that you will not take those "relationships" with you when you leave the team. This presents a huge challenge if you intend to build a "sphere of influence" of your own.

I have seen the "Team Model" work at a high level and I have seen it cause bitterness and strife. Here are some key things to consider before joining a team:

- What happens when you generate your own lead within the team? Is that subject to the same team terms and fees?
- Is there an exit agreement that clearly defines what happens to the business generated during your tenure with the team?
- Understand how the money works. Don't assume!

So many top producing agents are among the most generous people I know. Do your homework before joining a team, and recognize that you are not there to "GET" leads. You are a part of a team and "GIVE" your best toward achieving the goals of the team. If you select the right lead agent, they will create opportunities for you to grow and reward your efforts.

* You should consult an attorney before signing any agreement.

ESSENTIAL #2

Mastering the use of the Multiple Listing Service or MLS

This should be a short and straightforward conversation; however, the MLS is vastly different depending on your location.

Traditionally the MLS was controlled and facilitated by the local board of Realtors®. When the MLS went digital and then Realtor.com, Zillow and a host of other IDX (Internet Data Exchange) websites entered the scene we gave up our "keys to the kingdom." The agent "work product," listings, have somehow become public information. "Sold" data was always available to the public through tax data. The launch of Realtor.com brought a new dynamic making the agent work product public domain. That is ancient history now, but has left a legacy of a battle for relevance between Realtor® organizations, Multiple Listing Services, and Brokers. Like the children in an ugly divorce, Realtors® are left wondering who to trust, and with little choice in how these entities work together to resolve how to best serve agents that pay to keep all of them in business.

The most recent "Clear Cooperation" rule, implemented in 2020, has become a burden to agents and possibly damaging to consumers. Agents used to be able to market to a sampling of consumers prior to listing in the MLS. Having advanced showings before going "LIVE" in the MLS allowed sellers to test an optimistic price, finish a few last-minute improvements or acquire feedback as to whether they need to re-paint the purple living room. "Clear Cooperation" removes that option. This is just one example of where a service that was once designed to help agents and consumers has been twisted to serve entities struggling for relevance and power.

And, before I receive any hate mail, the "Clear Cooperation" rule also was instituted because during inventory shortages some brokers "hoard" their listings, market them on social media, put up signs and refuse to let other Realtors® show the property. These actions hurt sellers too by robbing them of exposure to the maximum buyer pool. Our job is always to serve the best interest of the consumer.

It is not the intention of this book to be political. Neutrality is good advice for "Real Estate Common Sense:" STAY AS NEUTRAL AS POSSIBLE REGARDING POLITICS OF ANY KIND! It may seem like this would be obvious, but there will be those that argue that taking a political view helps them connect with their community. It may also alienate you from potential buyers and sellers. Be authentic and true to your beliefs, and communicate them with respect for other's viewpoints.

Here is what I have to say about the MLS. Use it to the full. One way that new agents can shine is to really dig into the new and more technologically advanced features of the MLS. If you are a member of a Multiple Listing Service like Stellar MLS, the 3rd largest in the nation, then you have an abundance of tools at your fingertips.

Here are just some of the additional features of Stellar MLS that help agents serve buyers and sellers:

- ListTrac – A report that details views of listings on hundreds of real estate portals.
- Reverse Prospecting – A feature that allows a listing agent to communicate with agents that have a buyer with matching search criteria.
- Realist or iMapp – Detailed tax data, with multiple maps and comparable data.
- New Home Source – A resource for new construction listings.

This list could go on, but it changes often and is very specific to one MLS. Whether you take classes, view video tutorials, or just explore the additional features of the MLS, you can add value to your buyers and sellers by being able to use and articulate the benefits of the multiple tools and features of the MLS.

DIAMOND ASSIGNMENT

Ask 10 Top Agents what additional MLS features they use in their business.

ESSENTIAL #3
An Internalized Listing Presentation

If you are a "resister" of scripts and a doubter of prepared conversations, this will be a challenge for you. Seasoned agents can rely on their experience and sales record to influence sellers. As a new agent without that advantage, you will need advanced preparation.

In my experience, every seller wants to sell their home for the most amount of money in the least amount of time with the least inconvenience to them. For those of you who question whether there are three factors and not just one – price – I challenge you to review the iBuyer sales in your area. There are people that will risk the possibility paying more for service and selling for a lower price in order to save time and not be hassled with staging, showings and repair requests associated with the traditional real estate sale process.

If you work with a large brokerage you likely have a pre-constructed presentation available online or in print. Having attractive collateral for your conversation might be a helpful way of distinguishing your value. This material should also help you leverage the success of the agents in your office until you have a successful track record of your own.

Opinions vary on one stop or two stop listing appointments. There are occasions where there are zero stops and everything is conducted virtually. The following is information for you to consider, and then do what fits (or works) for you. If you do a lot of presentations without securing the listing, then look for a better "fit." Some of this might not make sense, or it may feel like too much work. Let your results guide you and try things that may be out of your comfort zone to increase your production. Here are 5 steps in the listing presentation:

Step 1 - The Interview

Here is where you get to know the needs of the consumer and their motivation for selling. This is where having a questionnaire at the ready will help. There is a balance between some "getting to know you" questions and interrogation. My opinion is that you should limit yourself to 10 questions. Here are my favorites:

1. Are you excited about your move?
2. When do you want (or have) to move?
3. What do you love about your home?
4. Are you speaking with anyone else; regarding, the sale of your home?
5. Have you thought about a price for your home?
6. How did you arrive at your price?
7. What are your major concerns about making a move?
8. What is most important to you?
   - Price
   - Timing
   - Convenience
9. What would it do to your plans if you decided not to sell?
10. When can we get together for me to take a look?

DIAMOND ASSIGNMENT

Review the 10 questions above, and modify them until they feel natural to you. Conduct the interview with 3 people and ask for feedback.

Step 2 - Tour the Home or Property

This is where the multiple-stop listing agents capture an advantage. These agents set a quick appointment ahead of time to tour the home and take measurements. They can also take a few key photos to use on the appointment with the decision makers.

If you are doing your tour at the time of the appointment with decision makers then you need to be polite, but do not spend too much time complimenting every aspect of the home. This will cloud your objective view of this property as a commodity that must be exchanged in a competitive environment.

Step 3 - Meeting with All Decision Makers

If "The Interview," referenced in step 1, was conducted in advance, and you are now in a face to face meeting, conference call, or video conference with any additional decision makers; repeat the interview questions with the following modifications:

Before asking the first question, ask: **"What do you expect from the real estate agent you choose to market and sell your home?"** Watch for confirmation of questions from your initial interview and get consensus from all of the decision makers so that you don't have to unnecessarily repeat any questions for your original contact.

Repeat your initial interview questions with a modification to the last question. You are now in front of all of the decision makers, so "when can we get together" doesn't make sense. Change your last question to "Are you ready to list your home today?"

By the end of your "Getting to Know You" questions, you should have built some rapport and practiced outstanding listening skills.

During these first three phases of the "Internalized Listing Presentation," you should have said nothing about you or your business, other than what may connect you to them or validate their responses. This is a big challenge for the gregarious personalities that are usually attracted to this "people business."

Step 4 - How you are going to find the buyer!

There are so many ways to describe what is going to happen next, but the focus of this conversation is on how you are going to find a buyer for their home.

You may have an elaborate presentation complete with sample marketing material. You may have marketing material already customized to their home (if you were one of those two-step appointment agents) that will draw them into the presentation because it is focused on them and their home.

Regardless of the length or detail of this phase, your task is to convince the seller that you have the tools and technology needed to cast a wide net for potential buyers.

Step 5 - Establish the "Offered At" Price

This is the last phase of the presentation. Please refrain from talking about price until you have worked through the other phases. If you launch into a pricing discussion too soon in the presentation you will never get to the rest of it. You will block their ears or break their hearts which is never a great place to start a relationship.

It is important to remember that it is the seller's decision. You are here to guide them to offer their home for sale at a price that will attract the right buyers. You do not know the value! That will be determined by a "ready, willing, and able" buyer and possibly an appraiser sent by the bank that will be financing it.

Your job is to explain the current pace and direction of the real estate market. This will be covered in detail in – Knowledge of the Local Real Estate Market on page 35. You will also use this opportunity to review your Comparative Market Analysis. I prefer to think of it as a "Competitive Market Analysis" because buyers search by comparison, and we need to position the price so it is the house they choose, so the CMA helps make the price competitive. By any other name the CMA is our tool to help sellers develop their offer to buyers. A more aggressive price will expand the buyer pool. A premium price will only attract buyers willing to pay a premium price; thereby limiting the buyer pool.

Your CMA can be an elaborate 3rd party production with embedded video, a presentation generated from a broker or MLS product or be a simple spreadsheet. The most important thing is to be comfortable with your research and your recommended price range. <u>Honor the seller with an honest evaluation.</u>

What did we forget to mention in the 5 steps of a listing presentation? Staging, compensation, professional photography? All of these should be covered after you decide to work together.

You may notice that the first 3 steps were for investigation, rapport building, and understanding the product you are marketing and your partners in the sale. "The Interview," "Touring the Property," and "Meeting with All of the Decision Makers" provide information about the experience you will have with the seller, or sellers. The 4th phase allows you to interview for the job. This sets the expectation with the sellers as to the experience you will be providing. And, step 5 is your first chance to work together in partnership on your new venture.

Once you have completed the 5 steps, memorialize your agreement with the listing paperwork. 100 additional conversations may occur, and many agents mess up the customer experience by bringing unnecessary process conversations in before the most important one. Do they want to work with you, and do you want to partner with them in selling their home? Once you answer that question, get the answer in writing.

Mega agents and large teams have mastered this. Your listing agreement should be completed with the compensation required for your marketing plan. Be prepared to discuss any questions or challenges to your plan calmly and knowledgeably. The way this relationship begins will set the tone for the entire process.

After you get the listing agreement signed and you are working through your marketing processes like, the photographer will be here on Friday, they may have an objection. That is why we keep the processes out of the presentation. Just give them the wonderful highlights of how your marketing plan gets them top dollar. Don't bog them down in the details until you know that you will be working together.

DIAMOND ASSIGNMENT

Prepare your foundational Listing Presentation and present 3 times to a family member, friend or pet. Remember to include all "5 Steps."

Step 1: Print your "Interview Questions" or set up an email template for digital delivery. Perhaps prepare a power point slide if you are planning virtual appointments?

Step 2: Look up the address. Print tax record information, the MLS data entry form, and what every history you can find on the property. Put on a clipboard with a blank cover page for notes as you tour the property. Confirm that the data you "pulled" matches what you are seeing.

Step 3: Treat this like a real meeting with all of the decision makers. The more you practice this, the better you will perform when it counts.

Step 4: Gather all of the information provided by your broker regarding available technology for promoting listings. Show how the technology you use helps them attract more buyers. Do you want to include print marketing or other unique marketing methods?

Step 5: Prepare and present a CMA.

"Put a bow on it!"

Complete all of the listing documents that are required by your state and your broker for your "practice" client.

ESSENTIAL #4

An Internalized Buyer Consultation

If you are "showing" property without first doing a buyer consultation, you are doing a great disservice to consumers and yourself. Purchasing a home is a process and, depending on the state, can have very strict timelines and requirements that must be met to stay compliant with the terms of the contract. Explaining this to potential buyers in advance will help them understand why their lender is "bugging" them for their w-2 and why you are insisting they decide if they want to request any repairs as a result of the home inspection, today!

Every transaction is unique, and there are a few roadblocks that occur frequently. These are the subjects we need to cover in our buyer consultation. Think of the buyer consultation as a way to explain your services and a way to determine the level of commitment of the buyer.

It is best to conduct a buyer consultation in the office. This can be problematic if you chose to associate with a broker that does not provide a brick and mortar location. A booth at a local coffee shop or another meeting place may be an alternative.

SAFETY NOTE

Open houses, meeting buyers at empty houses or remote locations are safety risks for Realtors®. Develop a policy that you apply to all potential clients. Making a copy of a driver's license and giving it to the receptionist is a good policy, but not if you single anyone out.

When I started my real estate career in 1994 it was customary to ride together for showings. For various reasons this has changed.

Regardless of customs in your area, always put your safety before a commission. Develop a safety plan. Our office knew someone was in trouble if they called and asked for "The RED folder." Safety first!

A buyer consultation is more curated than a listing presentation. You will want to adjust your consultation around local customs and processes as well as the individual preferences of the buyer.

The following is a list of suggested elements:

1. Needs Analysis
   - Where do they want to live?
   - What type of commute is acceptable?
   - Do they have a "center point" – Family, Friends, Recreation, Work, Worship?
   - Is there a preferred style of home?
   - When do they want to move?

2. Community Information

   This can be something as simple as a hand-drawn map of the areas you will be exploring or as elaborate as a collection of information and brochures from your local Chamber of Commerce. This is your chance to shine as "The Calm and Knowledgeable Guide." By developing your role as a valuable resource for information about the community you deepen your relationship with your clients. Your connection to the community will encourage communication beyond the sale. Future referrals depend on your continued relationship with the clients you have served. Remember to serve them well.

3. The Process

   Especially first-time homebuyers need the reassurance that you will shepherd them through the process of buying a home. Sharing a list of "Dos and Don'ts" or creating an illustrated timeline can reduce anxiety and show your value.

4. Pre-Approval

At the risk of being dogmatic, you must obtain a pre-approval early in the process. It will never get less awkward, so address financial qualification at your first meeting.

I also had a policy of "one free ride." If they did not arrive at our consultation with a pre-approval, we addressed it with the following question:

"Have you spoken with a mortgage lender to confirm your purchasing power?"

If they said yes, we were on our way. If they said no, I directed them to at least 3 lenders. It would also be wise to explain that all sellers have an expectation that we are touring their homes with qualified buyers, and shopping in the wrong price range leads to frustration for everyone.

5. Surprise and Delight

This is open to wide interpretation and an essential element in your consultation. A good laugh goes a long way. It can be as simple as a good clean, politically neutral, "fit for a 5th grader" joke. Or, you can shower your prospective buyer with branded notepads, magnets and other materials. A well-prepared itinerary, some water bottles and a smile can elevate the experience for the buyer.

DIAMOND ASSIGNMENT
Conduct 3 practice "Buyer Consultations."

DIAMOND ASSIGNMENT

Map the elements of your "Buyer Consultation" below:

ESSENTIAL #5

Knowledge of the Local Real Estate Market

Dedication to learning local real estate market statistics, the economic impact of area business growth, and understanding of the vision of local policymakers is a way that even newly licensed agents can shine.

Tap into resources early and often. Make going to planning board meetings, joining the local chamber of commerce, and reading local business publications a part of your routine. Or, at least *"google"* it . . . your customers are . . . and you don't want to be the last one to know that the biggest employer in the county is moving out of state.

Being "in the know" can be tricky. We want to be "the source of the source" and not be "the source." People don't want our opinion; they need facts. So, we should have lots of resources at our fingertips for school information, recreational facilities, and local permit and planning offices. And, we should direct our clients to those resources. Well-intentioned interpretation of information may influence a decision worth hundreds of thousands of dollars. If we missed something or misinterpret information, we could be opening ourselves up to litigation… YIKES!

Always remember this:

You are directing consumers to the information,

not providing the information.

Statistics, i.e. MATH, can be daunting for some. Many real estate boards publish pre-packaged statistical information. Contact your board or Multiple Listing Service to locate this information. Having accurate, up-to-date market information makes you much more interesting at parties, and will help build your reputation as a knowledgeable real estate professional. Always be prepared for the "how's the market" question with accurate data.

Published statistics usually take in a large area. Having state, county, and zip code real estate data is helpful, and sometimes we are called on to drill down into specific subdivisions or neighborhoods. "Absorption Rate" which is usually expressed as "Month's Inventory" is one of the key statistics in real estate.

"Absorption Rate" is used to determine the health of the real estate market in your area. Traditionally, the dividing line is 6 months inventory. When there is more than 6 months inventory, the market is referred to as a "Buyer's Market" and when there is less than 6 months inventory it is referred to as a "Seller's Market." It is the real estate industry measure of "supply and demand."

Here is my favorite way to bring consumers into the conversation about boring statistical information. For the following example, "indicators" is inserted instead of month's inventory or absorption rate, as "indicators" can cover a much broader statistics source. Establish some common ground by creating an agreement that most consumers rely on the media for their information. You could explain it this way:

> *"Many people rely on the media for real estate information, and the issue with this is that media trend reports lag behind the market. Additionally, the market lags behind the indicators. As a real estate professional, I am one of those agents that is "in" the market every day. I study the indicators and assist buyers and sellers in staying ahead of the market."*

Who doesn't want to be ahead? This conversation has allowed me to establish ongoing relationships as a valuable resource for people long after we complete a real estate transaction. I recently had someone I sold a home to 20 years ago ask me to evaluate an offer her son was making in another state. – Caution – As Realtors® we have a higher standard to meet and giving real estate advice in another state where a buyer is represented could be considered "tortious interference" and at the very least unprofessional behavior. I responded to her request by directing her to get valuation advice from her son's Realtor® and I shared some real estate "basics" with her.

We reviewed the photos and we had fun discussing how her son, who is now a doctor, couldn't possibly be old enough to purchase a home. One of the greatest rewards in having a real estate business is the people we meet along the way. This career has introduced me to interesting and extraordinary people I otherwise would have never met.

Wait… I promised not to turn this into a real estate memoir! Back to the subject at hand, "Absorption Rate."

The "Absorption Rate" is a measure derived from comparing the number of "like" homes for sale, against the number of "like" homes that have sold in the past 12 months. Here is the formula:

---

of *"Like"* homes SOLD in the last 12 months ÷ 12 = **X**

X = # of homes that "Sell" each month

of "Active Listings" ÷ **X** = Absorption Rate

This is the same formula that the Multiple Listing Service or Board of Realtors® is applying to establish the "months inventory." This formula is useful in establishing an offer price on unique properties or drilling down on properties located in large subdivisions. For the most part, you will be able to use the pre-designed statistics, and elevate your service above the "transactional" agents out there. So, let's talk about transactions.

 ## DIAMOND ASSIGNMENT

Go to the MLS and find how many homes sold in your zip code in the last 12 months. This is your "Like" homes. Now divide that number by 12. This is your "X" factor. Now how many active listings are in your zip code? Divide that number by your "X" factor. This is the absorption rate in your zip code!
You can continue to drill down with # of bedrooms, style of home, etc.

This page is for your absorption rate calculations:

ESSENTIAL #6

Transaction Management

Oh boy! Please forgive me for starting this chapter on my "soapbox." A cottage industry has developed from agents using "transaction coordinators" and there is absolutely a good argument for utilizing these services as your business volume builds. For crying out loud, for as long as you can, be the guide and constant communicator with your buyers and sellers. Too often agents hand off the transaction, communication, and unfortunately the relationship, to third party transaction managers. You may want to use a transaction manager to help you through your first few transactions, but I implore you not to turn over communication with your buyer or seller to anyone until you are so overwhelmed that you need relief. It is during the mundane almost daily communications throughout a transaction that we problem solve, recommend trusted vendors, and showcase our skill and experience. These interactions build trust, the most important factor determining future referrals.

The real estate transaction for **buyers** can be broken down as follows:

- Initial Consultation – Showing Homes
- Initiating and Negotiating the Offer
- Deliver Contract to ALL Parties- and your broker!
- Facilitating Inspections
- Negotiating Repairs
- Coordinating Mortgage, Survey and Title Services
- Monitoring Timelines of the Contract
- Assist with Closing Preparation
- Settlement – Servicing after the sale

* Remember to check with your broker for your local workflow systems and compliance requirements. Some states also customarily require attorneys to memorialize these processes.

The real estate transaction for **sellers** can be broken down as follows:

- Initial Consultation – Secure Listing
- Marketing – Systematized Marketing Plan
- Negotiating the Offer
- Deliver Contract to ALL Parties- and your broker!
- Facilitating Inspections
- Negotiating Repairs – Recommending vendors
- Coordinating Mortgage, Survey and Title Services
- Monitoring Timelines of the Contract
- Assist with Closing Preparation
- Settlement – Servicing after the sale

* Remember to check with your broker for your local workflow systems and compliance requirements

This is another area where the services offered by your broker matter. The real estate licensing exam does not prepare you for the complexity and interdependence of the multiple professionals involved the execution of a contract. As the Realtor®, you are the conductor on a train that depends on you to arrive at the destination on time and with everyone on board. Your performance will determine if the transaction runs smoothly on the tracks or is more like a runaway train careening into the station.

Your best offense is to READ THE CONTRACT! This sounds simple, and one of the biggest mistakes I have encountered in the last 20 years. The age of e-signatures has seemed to exacerbate this issue.

If you are a listing agent, carefully read the contract and addenda. If you are representing the buyer, you should have filled in the contract, and it is wise to review upon receipt in the event anything changed through negotiations. Many successful agents extract a timetable from the contract and enter into their google calendar. Some large firms have software that can do this as well.

Consult your Broker, mentor, or office compliance department for state, local and company policies and procedures!

ESSENTIAL #7

Having a Business Plan

As the saying goes, "If you fail to plan… you plan to fail." Making a business plan as a Realtor® presents a few challenges. First, we have to understand how our money is earned, then we have to calculate how the money is shared. We share our money with our co-op agents, we share our money with our brokers, we share our money with the government through taxes and we share our money with our family.

Money and the Math

Let's start with how the money is earned. If you are listing a home, you will likely charge a commission to the seller that will be shared with a cooperating agent or buyer's agent. You, the seller, and your broker will agree on the commission charged. I apologize for the vagueness of this explanation; however, it is an anti-trust violation to enter a specific amount here. You will have more control of your income if you are a listing agent. and many newer agents do more work with buyers.

So, let's say you listed a house and were paid a commission of "X" and you shared it with the buyer's agent at "Y." You split the commission with your broker at a " %" or a flat fee and you have a check in your hand for $4,000. This should be a conservative number, so check the math against your local market and adjust your plan accordingly. For our example we will use earnings of $4,000 per transaction.

The math looks something like this:

If the intention is to have an income (before taxes) of $100,000 per year then you will need to close 25 transactions per year. That is 2 transactions a month plus one surprise. Who doesn't love surprises? Easy… right?

Income Goal: $100,000

Average Check: $4,000

$100,000 ÷ $4,000 = 25 Transactions

According to the National Association of Realtors®, the median gross income of REALTORS® was $41,800 in 2018. This means that most agents are not making the mark of 2 transactions per month, or they live in a part of the country where the median sale price is low, or they are paying a lot to their broker. Regardless of the cause, it is important to understand what is realistic.

Developing a SMART Business Plan

The acronym S.M.A.R.T. has been used for so many for so long, that I am not sure who should get credit for it? We will use it here, because it is still relevant. *(S = Specific, M=Measurable, A=Attainable or Achievable, R = Realistic or Relevant and T= Time-Bound or Timely. When I am teaching, I like to add Y=YOURS!)* There is no point in having a plan forced on you by your broker or coach. If it is not your plan, you are not likely to execute it. Take some time to fully explore the SMARTY Plan.

S – Specific

Your plan should have specific goals that can be checked on regularly to measure your progress. One of my favorite tools as a coach was to track goals with a "Needle Mover" guide. *(The needle mover guide can be found in the appendix or on www.RealEstateCommonSense.com)* If your goal is not easily defined by contacts made, contracts written, transactions completed, and ultimately income generated, your goal is not specific enough.

M – Measurable

This is where a study of "The 4 Disciplines of Execution" by Chris McChesney is recommended. There are lots of youtube videos related to "The 4 Disciplines of Execution" if you don't want to read the book; and here we want to explore lag and lead measures.

If I want to lose 50 lbs. that is a lag measure. The lead measures are calories burned and calories consumed. The results are different for some people, but the principle remains the same. Our lead measures for real estate are conversations and appointments, and our lag measures are contracts written and income earned. For a successful business plan, measure both lag and lead measures.

A – Attainable or Achievable

To quote the motivational speakers out there, "everything is attainable." Any of us that are parents want our children to live in a world of opportunity and unlimited possibilities. Real estate is a world of opportunity, and we have to grow into the unlimited possibilities before us. Many agents have left the business because they had an unrealistic expectation of how quickly they could attain their goals. The internet changed some dynamics with the ability to "purchase" leads. This is a quick way to run up debt, and unfortunately, I have seen many agents leave defeated and in debt. Take some time to consider how to play "the long game." Highly successful agents build a referral business over the years, one happy client at a time.

R – Realistic or Relevant

This portion of the plan relates to the direction and pace of your market. If prices are climbing in a community with a robust economy and home sales are brisk, then it is realistic to be optimistic about your plan. If there is little movement in your market, prices are declining or there is an economic disruption in your community, then you may need to adjust your expectations? If you have a budget to meet adjusting your expectations doesn't mean reduce your income goal. It means you will have to get to that goal with a more vigorous plan. For instance, I learned that I would always work harder in election years. The uncertainty slowed the market, every time. Could this experience be unique to me?

T – Timely or Time-Bound

This one is interesting, as year after year I see business planning events in December and January. Too late! In my opinion September is the best time to do a real estate business plan for the calendar year ahead. There is at least a 90-day "ramp-up" period to most real estate production, so include that in the time calculation.

Here is a super simple business plan for your first year in real estate:

Specific Goal: Make $100,000 by having 25 transactions

Measures: Attempted Contacts

Contacts Made

Leads Obtained

Appointments Made / Executed

Contracts Written

Measures need to be, well … measured, so put the letters ACLAC vertically on a calendar and start counting – You may even want to have two columns. One for your goal and the other for actual:

A – Attempts

C – Conversations

L – Leads

A – Appointments

C – Contracts Written

The **"A"** is every time you **attempt** a contact. Are you calling? Visiting in person? Or, sending letters? **"C"** is where you record how many **conversations** you were able to have. Next year you will appreciate having a record of what types of conversations brought you the most leads. **Leads** are tricky. Represented by **"L,"** for me, a lead is someone I like who will benefit my business now or in the future. This will hurt your ratio of leads to appointments, but I feel brings better results in the long run. You may choose to narrow your definition of a lead. The second **"A"** can sometimes be divided into **Appointments** made and Appointments executed. There can be an occurrence of appointments set that are not kept. You may not need to do that if you are focused on referral-based appointments. They rarely cancel. Lastly, the second **"C"** is for the **contracts** written. These are listing agreements or buyer representation agreements. If you do not want to adopt these, take some time to develop your own "lead measures."

Your lag measures, contracts closed and income; will be measured in your bank account! Or, create the "10 Minute Business Plan" referenced below. Most of your planning will occur around the "measures" portion of your business plan.

Attainable: What do you need to confidently write a contract today, perhaps it is training or a tool? Get it and get started.

Realistic: Use statistics from the MLS to confirm

Timely: Give yourself 90 Days to ramp up then set a time frame in which you want to accomplish your goals.

Yours: Don't use my numbers unless they are yours.

For years I have helped agents launch their careers with a simple "10 Minute Business Plan" which incorporates Goal Setting, Time Blocking and Prospecting. The reason most people don't follow a business plan, if they have one, is that they are too complicated. Keep it simple, look at it often, and celebrate your milestones and victories.

DIAMOND ASSIGNMENT

Complete a business plan.

The following resources can be found under the "Business Builders" Navigation button at: www.RealEstateCommonSense.com

"Goal Setting Using Needle Movers"

"The 10 Minute Business Plan"

"Easy Prospecting Plan"

See appendix starting on page 81 for samples of documents

List your S.M.A.R.T.Y. business plan below:

ESSENTIAL #8

Marketing, Technology, and Social Media

Once again, we have saved the best for last! There is not enough room, nor do I have the expertise to dive deep here. This will be an attempt to simplify what can be a very complicated process. Most importantly marketing, social media and other technology designed to support your real estate business can quickly become a "black hole" that diverts your time away from important revenue-producing real estate activities.

From the perspective of someone that has managed a real estate career through a Palm Pilot to a Blackberry to an iPhone, the best advice on technology is stay curious and adopt what works for you. We want to be on "the cutting edge," not "the bleeding edge."

The next few pages will decidedly deal with broad descriptions, designed to provide a structure or outline for your customized plan. Your plan should be examined every year and modified to reflect current trends, new offerings, and changes in social media algorithms.

The intended audience for this book is newer or striving agents that are looking for guideposts, so this section will have an analysis component. We will list the marketing item, technology, or social media strategy then you should take a moment to analyze it. Several passes were made to keep the subject current, and yet incorporate some tried and true methods that are still producing results for agents.

The following charts are designed to provide clarity around where to spend your most valuable resource – your time and energy! If your broker is providing a website for you then you could consider 4 options. The first is "provided by my broker" and move on. Option 2 is that you want a personal customized presence online and you have the skill and time to invest in making it just right. There are also many website designers out there and you may choose to hire a 3rd party. That would be your 3rd option. Lastly, you may decide that you can't address a website right now. You would exercise the 4th option to address it in the future. It is possible to select multiple options.

The overlap between marketing, technology and social media made it impossible to review them independently, so we divided them by "Marketing Your Business," "Marketing for Buyers," and "Marketing for Sellers." There is also emerging technology that will assist you with the transaction; however, transaction compliance varies so much from state to state, that it has been omitted from the analysis. We have also left some blank space for your unique value proposition or specializations.

How to use the charts:

B: Provided by the broker

S: Personal commitment to design and maintain

O: Provided by a 3rd party (MLS, Paid Service, etc.)

F: Something that will be incorporated in the future.

Marketing Your Business	B	S	O	F
Launch Announcement – Press release, print advertising or letter/postcard				
Website or Landing Page				
Professional/Permanent email address				
Business Cards				
Name Badge				
Listing and Open House Signs				

Marketing Your Business	B	S	O	F
Brochure or Outline of Services				
Monthly Newsletter or Postcard Campaign				
Facebook Personal Profile / Business Page				
Linked-in Profile				
Youtube Channel				
Other: Instagram, Twitter, etc.				
Podcast / Video Studio				

Marketing Services for Buyers	B	S	O	F
Home Search App				
Buyer Representation Agreement				
Buyer Consultation Digital or Print				
System for capturing interested buyers from listings				
First Time Buyer or Investor Workshops				
Interest Rate/Down-payment Assistance/ Specialty Financing Social Media Posts				
Open House Plan Digital or Printed				
Neighborhood, City or Regional Information for Relocation Clients				

Marketing Services for Sellers	B	S	O	F
Seller Presentation Digital or Print				
Lockbox and Showing Tracking				
Customizable Marketing Plan				
"Just Listed" Campaign				
Social Media "Boosting"				
#Hashtag Campaign				
Listing Photos				
Virtual Tour				
Brochure – Digital or Print				
Home Warranty				
Seller Disclosure				
Postcard Campaign				
Circle Prospecting/Radius Marketing				
Listing Website/Landing Page				
Scheduling/Feedback Service				
Specialized Print Advertising				
Listing Internet Activity Tracking				
Reverse Prospecting				

* Additional customization here is your chance to highlight your unique talent.

Marketing Services for both Buyers and Sellers	B	S	O	F
Transaction Management Plan				
Neighborhood Newsletter / Website				
Social Media Real Estate Market Updates				
CRM – Customer Relationship Manager				

These charts are by no means a comprehensive list. They are intended to provide focus. They are also a way for you to evaluate and appreciate some of the systems and services provided by your broker. You may be launching your business with a unique niche. Perhaps a builder has hired you to market their properties? You could be associated with a brokerage or team that specializes in foreclosures? It is my hope that this structure will inspire your creative process, and that I have outlined some customary services so that buyers and sellers can have a better consumer experience.

Marketing, Technology and Social Media - The Budget

Creating a separate bank account for your real estate business allows you to monitor your budget. Tax time will be much easier if all of your income and expenses related to your real estate business are in one place. Using a dedicated credit card only documents expenses. Keeping everything separate from your personal funds will aide in your growth and as you grow you may want to incorporate for tax savings. Consult with a tax advisor before doing this. It is not always the right decision.

The chart below is a template with sample entries to demonstrate the importance of working from a budget. As with all budgets the first entry should be what you intend to spend. Our recommendation is that, whenever possible, you combine personal marketing with listing promotion for better economy.

Here are a few items to consider:

Membership fees for networking groups, social media "boosting" budget, professional photographer/videographer, print collateral, open house promotion, leveraged services (telemarketing services, intern, marketing assistant)

Budgeted Item	Budget	Spent	Balance
			$5000.00
Branded Signs	$500.00	$200.00	$4800.00
Promotional Items	$1000.00	$700.00	$4100.00
Networking Activities	$500.00	$300.00	$3800.00
Listing Promotion	$1000.00		
Photographer with Drone		$350.00	$3450.00
Social Media Boosting	*$20/boost*	$200.00	$3250.00
Postcard Campaign		$500.00	$2750.00
Electronic Lockbox		$150.00	$2600.00
... you get the idea			

Jot down your budget basics:

THE CONVERSATION

We could stop the book after the "8 Real Estate Essentials" with confidence you have what you need to launch your career. Somehow there is always hesitation on where to begin. "What if I don't know what to say, or what if the buyer or seller asks ……." are often the fears of the newer agents. It all starts with a conversation.

I have attended the course "Fierce Conversations" with multiple facilitators, and I highly recommend it. I had the privilege to attend a presentation by the author, Susan Scott. My notes below may include personal interpretation, and the following words are what I recorded in my journal and are indelibly fixed in my mind.

"Life is a conversation; it requires two components: someone to speak and someone to hear. The prefix 'con' denotes 'with.' To be 'with' someone in a conversation requires empathy, patience, and a willingness to put aside self-interest. We spend so much time in 'versations' that our lives circle endlessly without results."

Sadly, some Realtors® have not earned a reputation for displaying empathy, patience and the putting aside of self-interest. Yet, I assure you, if you can enter each conversation with those qualities you will have a highly successful career ahead of you.

We are at a crossroad where we can conclude this book wishing you well. Or, share the conversations that I have had over the years. The words that work. The dreaded scripts that produce results. Most importantly we want to acknowledge that scripts are not designed to manipulate or deceive. They are designed to address the common issues that consumers experience. By using a script we can address issues in a concise, confident and truthful manner.

Remember to invite consumers into the conversation. The script is simply a framework to keep the conversation moving in a productive direction; and provide a new perspective for the buyer or seller. If you ever leave your role as a calm and knowledgeable guide by the conversation escalating in intensity or accusation, it is time to stop talking. Refrain from defending your position and recognize the need to pause. This pause will give you time to hear, appreciate, and understand a new perspective. You may not reach an agreement, but you will leave the conversation knowing you gave the person with you space for their opinion and acknowledged their self-expression, and you will have protected the relationship. Being seen and heard is powerful. Infusing others with power builds relationships. Building your library of scripts helps you set standards for your business so that "infusing others with power" doesn't mean giving up your own.

Let me, once again, be clear. Scripts are simply words that work. They help us navigate common and recurring events. If you are afraid of being mechanical or too rehearsed, consider the words "I love you." Arguably three of the most overused, misinterpreted, and sometimes abused words in the English language. Yet, how many of us require those words, value those words, and have even created new iterations to make them unique to our own relationships?

It is because the words "I love you" work! They can calm us, excite us, and even produce results. Here we will share some additional "words that work" to calm us, excite us and produce results.

Words that work

Lead Generation – Super Simple Scripts

Hi, I'm a Realtor®, what do you do?

This script resulted in 3 transactions for my friend Chris. He asked the question of a total stranger at a cruise terminal. Thank you, Chris, for this simple, straight-forward, and effective script.

When can we meet?

When can we get together to discuss …

Lead Generation - Sphere of Influence:

As your REALTOR I want to make sure I am providing you with all of the real estate-related services you need. Did you receive the "Market Update" I sent last week? Is there anything else I could do to provide better service?

OR

I am calling to ask for your help... Can I count on you for one referral this year? Is there anything I can do to help you achieve your goals this year?

Lead Generation - Open House:

How did you hear about our open house? . . . reply . . . Was there something particular about this house or neighborhood that interested you? . . . point to sign in sheet or electronic sign in app... If you sign in here, I would love to help you find your perfect home.

OR

Are you a neighbor or are you looking to buy a home?

* Remember to make neighbors feel welcome and treat them as a special invited guest. They may be interviewing you for the job of listing their home.

Lead Generation - Affiliated Professionals:

Do you have a referral buddy that is handling your real estate needs? If not, I would like to get together for coffee to see how we might be able to help each other.

We could get together Wednesday at 9 or would Monday at 8 work better for you?

* Anecdotal observation: When scheduling an appointment, offer your preferred time first. Then your second option is an available "closer" appointment time. The pressure of the closer time will usually make them choose your preferred time. Also, offering a two-choice appointment increases the "yes" response.

Lead Generation - Other Realtors:

> As an agent that I admire and respect I was calling to ask if you may have any times where you are unable to follow up on all of the leads your listings generate? I am willing to work any leads you send me and give you a XX% referral fee.

Lead Generation - Door Knocking:

> As a REALTOR that specializes in this neighborhood, I wanted to stop by and share (real estate statistical report, sports calendar, school calendar etc.) and also to share some recent sold data for your neighborhood. Many people rely on websites like Zillow. Aside from the margin for error these "zestimates" don't acknowledge the special features of your unique property. If you do not have a Realtor®, I would love to offer my services, to keep you up to date with more accurate information.

Lead Generation - Your Favorites:

Call In – Request for Showing:

> Agent: Will this be an investment or your homestead property?

> Cust: Why do you ask?

> Agent: There are special programs and incentives for homestead properties in the state of Florida. Can I have your name and number in the event we get disconnected while I look up that property?

* If your state does not have homestead exemptions then focus the conversation on any unique considerations for purchasing a home in your state. This is your opportunity to show that purchasing a home with a Realtor® is so much more than just showing homes. We are a calm and knowledgeable guide!

Pre-Approval:

> Have you spoken with a mortgage lender to confirm your purchasing power?

> * You may want to add:

> Aggressively priced homes in any market sell within days. If you see a house you love, we need to be prepared to move quickly. Confirming your purchasing power now puts you in a position to win.

Come into The Office – CITO (Or Schedule a Video Conference)

> When can you come into the office so that we can talk about some of the advantages, pitfalls, and special considerations about buying a home in ……… I would also like to update you on our current market conditions so that you can have an advantage during negotiations. Is _____ or _____ better for you.

OR

I will call and get that appointment set up immediately… when can you come into the office so that we can get you out to see that home? *(we will meet you there)* I will have to call the other agent and schedule the showing. While I am doing that, I will also find some other options for you to consider, so that you can make a good decision. Wouldn't you agree that buying a home is an important decision? Let's get you positioned to make buying a home a huge win for you.

Come into The Office – CITO (Or Schedule a Video Conference)

I would love to show you that property. Can you … come into the office … on ---------------- at ---------- or would ----------- at --------------- be better?

Cust: Can't you just meet me at the property?

Agent: Have you ever heard the name, Beverly Carter?

Agent: I could meet you at the property if I did not care about my personal safety or delivering the best service to my customers. You see, if you will take just 20 minutes of your time to meet me in the office, I can go over some important information and strategies that help my customers get the properties they desire at the lowest possible price. Would --------------- at ----------- work for you?

* Beverly Carter is a Realtor® who made national headlines when she lost her life by meeting a stranger at a vacant house in 2014. It was a wake-up call for all of us. There is also some argument that in office buyer consultations are not practical. Regardless of whether you have a "brick and mortar" office, you should meet potential buyers in a neutral location for your safety. A video conference option would be to screen shot the potential buyer's driver's license. Your safety policy should be applied to EVERY potential buyer in order to not violate fair housing regulations.

Contract Signing:

Now, have you ever made an important decision like this before? You remember, as soon as you make the decision, all kinds of thoughts start running through your head. You will start asking your friends and family to support your decision, and you know how some people are. They love to just pick everything apart. They were not with us through this process. Don't let them make you doubt your decision. And, if you think of something that concerns you, please call me so that we can work through it together. I'm on your side, I am here to support you, and to be your advocate.

Home Inspection:

Were you ever engaged? Well, you and this home have been engaged. After our inspection today, it will be like you have been married for 2 years. You will find out all the bad habits, hidden secrets, and little bonuses. The purpose of the inspection today is to see if there is something structurally wrong, or some other undisclosed defect, not to make the house perfect. Just like our spouse, we learn to love them flaws and all.

PLEASE NOTE: "The inspection period" in a contract is a highly emotional time, and it is imperative that your clients feel you are their advocate. The classic "buyer's remorse" also emerges during this time. Special attention should be given to your buyers. If they feel that you have shifted sides by minimizing their concerns, they may quietly find another Realtor® to show them properties. The midnight email saying "we found another house this weekend" is a heartbreak. It may feel awkward, but if you sense that they are doubting their purchase, you should offer to help them. The re-assurance that you want them to find the right house, even if it is not this one, goes a long way. Most of the time, they don't take you up on it, and they do appreciate the offer.

Multiple Offer Situation:

Cust: I don't want to bid against myself. . . Why can't we find out what the other offers are?

Agent: While it is understandable that you don't want to bid against yourself, the seller also wants to get the best price possible so they don't give any of their equity away. The only way for any of us to know what this house is worth is to find out what a ready, willing and able buyer pays for it at closing.

Let's do this:

I want you to close your eyes, and fast forward to 3 months from now.

You did not make an offer on this house

You are sitting at your computer, and you look at the tax appraiser's website.

You see this house on your screen with the sale price recorded.

What number makes you say: "I would not have paid that for that house!"

What number makes you say: "I would have gladly paid that!"

Don't be carried away with the thrill of the chase. Ultimately a house is only worth what a ready, willing, and able buyer is willing to pay for it . . . Let's make an offer . . .that could make you that buyer!

* A buyer is much less stressed during a multiple offer situation if you took the time to begin their home search with a buyer consultation that reviewed the pace and statistics of the local real estate market. If you wait to explain the market until after they have selected a "hot property," they may resist your suggestions to be aggressive with their offer.

Helping Sellers Set an "Offered At" Price

Allowing a seller to "test the market" when it favors buyers can cause the seller to miss the best price. We bear a heavy responsibility when we are in a "buyer's market" because time is an enemy when prices are on the decline. The best price, when inventory is outpacing sales, is obtained immediately. Delivering disappointing news in your pricing analysis is difficult and necessary. Be honest and firm.

It was always a best practice for me to not hone in on a specific price, but rather offer a range that included what I thought was the ideal "Offered At" price. The low end of the range is referred to as the wholesale price, and the upper number the retail price. Most sellers will gravitate to the upper range. This opens up the opportunity to talk about that number being the "perfect" number. The perfect number is only obtained when a home in perfect condition meets an ideal buyer. *(Ideal buyer script on page 11)*

When we are in a "seller's market" less damage is done in testing the market. However, it is still imperative to provide accurate pricing data. There are a lot of opinions, but only one set of facts. Refine your CMA skills. Being overly optimistic on price can cause distress even in a seller's market. An anxious buyer willing to make an offer outside of the range of your CMA, usually includes an appraisal contingency. The appraisal, if lower than the offer price, can trigger re-negotiation and anxiety for the seller.

One of the top producing agents in our office shared this amazing script with her sellers to set expectations around appraisal surprises:

Setting Expectations Regarding Appraisals:

> In our area over 80% of home sales require financing. This means that even if we find a buyer that is willing to pay over our asking price *(which had become common in the highly desirable community this agent specialized in)* we may have to make adjustments after appraisal. The great thing about when this happens, is we are assured we didn't leave one penny of your equity on the table! – *Thank you, Kat White, for this winning script.*

Explaining Pricing Strategy:

> We will not know the sale price until we have a ready, willing, and able buyer close on your home. And remember, none of us can achieve our goal unless we get to a signed contract that leads to a successful closing.

> Pricing is the window through which buyers search for a home. Marketing is only effective when we are in the right window. Pricing is a part of marketing.

A "Buyer's Market"

> Listing your home in a buyer's market is like entering a price war and a beauty contest, and I am here to help you win both.

> We want to price ahead of the competition so that we don't have to chase the market as it contracts. We may also need to improve the condition so we get the attention of the best buyers.

> Additional sales in a buyer's market work against sellers. Capturing a buyer now gives us the best chance at preserving your equity.

Modified "Buyer's Market" for seller wanting a retail price

> Listing your home at the highest retail price is like entering a price war and a beauty contest, and I am here to help you win both.

> We will need to compete with ideal homes "as seen on HGTV." The condition of the home should be model home quality, so we get the attention of the best buyers.

> Buyers will expect to have a high-end experience that reflects our high-end price.

A "Seller's Market"

Wow… that price is above the recommended range. In a seller's market, we can be optimistic, and I am the most optimistic Realtor in our area.   I have an aggressive marketing plan, and I am positive we can get you the best price.

Even in a Seller's Market, we can miss the window where buyers looking for a home like yours are searching. That may put getting the BEST PRICE at Risk.

May I explain?

Let's say it is January and you are shopping for a sweater. You walk into your favorite retail store …… *(let them name it)*

There is the perfect sweater! What are you willing to pay for the sweater …. *(they name the amount… we will use $50 for our example)*

So, you look at the tag on the sweater and you see $200.00. Are you buying a sweater today? *(they may or may not respond)*

Now you return to the store in March and the sweater is now $100. And, you are in the market for a $50 sweater, so you pass again.

In April you return to the store and on the clearance rack at the back of the store, is the sweater you have been admiring. And, LOOK it is now $50. It is not as well presented as the first day you saw it. You know the "picked over" look that sweaters get. You may wonder why other people didn't buy the sweater. It may even have a lipstick stain or pull in it from someone else trying it on. Now it is also getting warmer, you may not even need a sweater any more.

How much will you pay? If you are like most people you may take it to the register and ask for an additional discount, since it is a "leftover."

Unfortunately, the same thing happens with homes that linger on the market. Buyers then tend to make lower offers because they feel no one else wanted the house. Testing the market above our recommended range can be dangerous.

A Transitioning or Recovering Market or when portions of the market are an anomaly.

We have to be very strategic about pricing when we are in recovery, a transition, or situation with a pricing anomaly.

Pricing is the window through which we market your home. __XX__ homes sold last month in the $XXX,XXX price range. There are currently __XX__ for sale. The ratio between the number of homes sold and the number of homes available is how we determine whether we are in a buyer or seller's market.

The strategy is to price in line with recent sales and slightly below the current competition. There are several homes that a buyer may choose, and we need to be keenly aware of the perception of the abundance of supply with low demand.

Ultimately, it is your home, and only you can determine what price will accomplish our goal of selling your home, and what selling this home means to you.

We are not responsible for the market. We are the calm and knowledgeable guide operating in the market of the moment.

Seller Conversations in a Seller's Market	Seller Conversations in a Buyer's Market

DIAMOND ASSIGNMENT

Make 5 lead generation "Seeking New Business" calls and record your results here. Ask your broker, mentor or top agent to review them with you. Record some new "Words that Work."

As Realtors® we should know our local inventory. The best homes sell quickly regardless of the market. Most buyers will request to see properties they have seen online. If you are not doing your homework, it shows. Before you leave your consultation, you should be able to tell them, that you are honoring their request for showings, but house "A" has a railroad track directly behind it, and house "B" faces a strip mall.

This last script or technique added a minimum of $20,000 per year to my income. If you can add a well-priced attractive home to the itinerary of every buyer you are working with, you will increase your sales.

Here is the 5 Step process for building relationships and closing more sales by elevating the buyer experience with the "Best Home" system.

The "Best Home" System:

Step 1: Do you mind if I add one more property to our itinerary today? This will help me determine if I am clear on exactly what you are looking for, and help you see that I am the best Realtor to help you find a home.

Step 2: Show them the "best" home you could find in their price range.

Step 3: Have a conversation with them about what works, and what doesn't work, about the "best" home.

Step 4: If it is your day for a miracle, they love the "best" home and want to make an offer. More often they will help you by sharing where you think alike. Remember you just showed them what you think is the "best" home available in their price range. Let them share what they think would be needed to make the "best" home a "perfect" home.

Step 5: Call them when the next home that includes their "perfect" features comes on the market. You could start your conversation: "When can we get out to see the perfect home?" OR "I found the 'perfect' property for you."

If your "best" homes sell quickly, then you are good at this. You will get good at finding gems, and that is what buyers are looking for in their Realtor®!

DIAMOND ASSIGNMENT

Search the MLS for the "Best Home" in your areas of specialization, preview them (if possible) and add the appropriate one to your next buyer showing in that area.

Week 1:

Price Range	Address	MLS #
Under $200k		
$200k-$250k		
$250k-$300k		
$300k-$350k		
… and so on…		

Week 2:

Price Range	Address	MLS #
Under $200k		
$200k-$250k		
$250k-$300k		
$300k-$350k		
… and so on…		

Week 3:

Price Range	Address	MLS #
Under $200k		
$200k-$250k		
$250k-$300k		
$300k-$350k		
… and so on…		

Track your results … if your "Best Home" is still available after 3 weeks, it is not a "Best Home." Re-evaluate your "picking" skills.

The most important conversation:

This chapter cannot be concluded without the most important element of any conversation, honesty! There is a trap that is set when we are "the guide" that leads us to share what we think we know. Buyers and Sellers do not want to know what we think, they want accurate and truthful information supported by facts.

When we are asked a question, our ego demands that we answer quickly and with confidence. Train yourself to pause and reflect on what you really know. If you are relying on the MLS data, let them know. It is not always correct. If you are making an educated guess, then be sure to preface your comment as such. This script will help you, and I recommend you use it in as many variations as possible.

"I am not 100% sure about the answer to that question, would you like me to do some research?"

This simple, yet powerfully honest script will prevent you from rushing to give opinion over fact. Your integrity is on the line when you rush to provide information.

Be a resource for "all things real estate" in your community. Service the transaction as an advocate for your client, and follow up on all service as a way to protect the relationship. Always protect the relationship! In the end your business is built by the relationships you nurture, protect and enhance throughout your career.

More space for your "words that work":

THE 100 DAY PRODUCTIVITY PLAN

The biggest challenge as a broker is the 1ˢᵗ 100 days. Sadly, a huge percentage of Realtors® leave the profession within the first two years. After a decade of interviewing, training, and supporting agents, we know that productivity is the one thing that will give agents the best shot at sustaining their careers. It sounds simple, but it is not easy. There are a lot of distractions and ancillary businesses built on selling agents the "snake oil" of instant success.

One of the most attractive elements of being a Realtor® is the dynamic and intriguing environment. Surprises are a part of the daily routine, and regardless of how much time you spend preparing, no two transactions are the same. You are going to have to be a master problem solver and a person confident in taking action.

The next few pages will attempt to outline the 1st 100 days in a way that move you into productivity quickly and responsibly. You will also notice an intentional overlap. Launching your career is like jumping into a moving "double-dutch" jump rope. Your board orientation may be required before you can obtain a lockbox key app and so on. Too many agents waste their first few months getting ready to get ready. Hopefully you have chosen a broker with a mentor program or training support. Lean into it!

Day 1

Assuming that you researched, interviewed and selected a broker; As soon as you have your license in hand, or the promise of one in the mail, head to your broker and complete your onboarding process.

Days 1-10 (Registration and Orientation)

Days 1-10

Get your checkbook or credit card ready to see some action. It is time to pay for your board dues (if required), MLS membership, and lockbox key app. You may also need to buy electronic lockboxes, signs and business cards. Sometimes lockboxes, signs and business cards are provided by your broker.

Days 1-30 (Training and Skill Building)

Days 1-30

This book should be a good resource for your 1st 30 days. You need to plug in to any resources you have locally that help you develop the regional or state specific adaptations of the "Real Estate Essentials" outlined on pages 5-8.

In addition to an internalized listing and buyer consultation you will also need to master the skill of hosting an open house. Practice your consultation with your spouse, your kids, your mom and then your dog until all of them are tired of it. Do not practice on buyers and sellers. Attend open houses hosted by experienced agents every weekend in your first 30 days.

Day 1 – Forever (Building a Database)

Day 1- Forever

From your 1st day in real estate you have one key focus: "To build a database of potential clients." You can hope to attain a magic number of 10, 20 or 100,000 people in your database or you can adopt a brave and efficient way of building your business.

There are not a lot of books out there advocating this, but it worked for me at a high level. It is the "Fair Trade" method. Your goal in building your database is to find 100 people that will commit to sending you at least one buyer or seller referral a year.

Then, and this is the part that most people won't do, commit to activities that help them. If they own a business, then send them business. If they lead a charity, help them raise money for their charity. Be a friend. Not a social media friend. The real kind that takes them to lunch and knows the names of their kids and sends them a card when their dog dies. If each of your top 100 send you one referral each year, and you convert 50% of them into viable business, you will have a business that will sustain you and an assistant in most parts of the country.

In your first weeks, go through your phone and have conversations like this:

> I have just started a career in real estate and I am looking for 20 people that may be able to refer a buyer or seller to me this year.
>
> Thanks mom

Days 1-60 (Adopt Technology Tools)

Days 1-60

You have started a database and it is time to employ the marketing, technology and social media tools listed on pages 48-52. It may seem like a good idea to just put your new contacts in your phone because you can rely on your instant recall superpower. Trust that this method is not sustainable. A spreadsheet and loose-leaf notebook were what I started with, but you will likely want to use a CRM – Customer Relationship Management System. Some brokers provide them, others encourage using what may be provided by your MLS. There are also tons of third-party CRM providers ranging from free to thousands of dollars a month.

Real estate technology tools are also available in abundance and create analysis paralysis or cause you to go into debt by falling for the "silver bullet" or "magic pill" that provides closed sales with the push of a button. In my opinion, you will be better served if you keep it simple for now.

During your first 100 days focus on building relationships with potential customers, vendors and fellow Realtors®. Then dedicate some time to the following technologies:

- Master the MLS and its additional features
- Set up your Social Media pages
- Engage in the technology offered by your broker

There are hundreds of things you can do. There are a few things you must do, there is power in focusing on the real estate essentials.

Days 30 – 60 (5 Appointments or Open Houses)

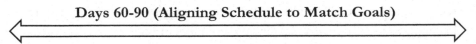

Days 30-60

Start hosting Open Houses either virtual or in person. Prospect for business and trust that the dedicated time you spent preparing will help secure contracts. If you took a passive approach to your first 30 days and did not explore your tools by writing "test" contracts and rehearsing with friends and family, you will be practicing with customers when you should be performing. Your results will reflect your investment. Buyers and sellers deserve performance not practice.

Days 60-90 (Aligning Schedule to Match Goals)

Days 60-90

It is time to develop a strategy and build a business plan. How many days a week will you dedicate to your new business? Take away the judgement around it and be honest about what you intend to accomplish. Did you begin this career to have more time with your family? A flexible schedule does not mean that your workweek consists only of the 2 or 3 appointments with buyers and sellers. If you went to a restaurant for a meal, you would not expect a food service professional to dump the raw ingredients of your meal on the table. Likewise, your clients expect you to serve a well-prepared experience delivered with some style. Set your schedule to reflect your goals!

Google calendar works great for time blocking and you can attend an abundance of time blocking workshops including one that I facilitate a couple of times a year. *(The 10 Minute Business Plan)* In the end, your schedule should be blocked at least a month in advance and include personal time, lead generation time, training and growth time, and enough white space to accommodate new opportunities as they arise.

Days 90-100 (Reflection and Focus)

⟵――――――――――――――――――――――――――⟶

Days 90-100

Sometime toward the end of your 100 days, schedule a family meeting, and then a few hours for quiet reflection of your first 100 days. Has your family adapted to your new routine? Did you get caught in any of the deadly "bunny trails" that delayed the launch of your business? If so, talk to one of your bosses. Was it Me, Myself or I who wasn't focused on building a business?

Therein lies the challenge of being an entrepreneur. Sometimes we are too hard on ourselves, or the opposite. Sometimes those that left a career that demanded a lot of time and energy have a rebound response and coast into their new routine. If you were too easy on yourself, hit the reset button and work your way through this book again. If you were too hard on yourself with unrealistic goals, or taking on too many tough clients, then take a deep breath and evaluate where you had fun and where you experienced success. For so many of us, success and fun are closely linked.

Buyers and sellers want to be served by enthusiastic and engaging professionals. If you are not having fun, your clients will feel it. That does not mean your first 100 days will be smooth sailing. "A smooth sea never made a skillful sailor." So, expect to have challenges, especially in the first 100 days. How have you been doing with those challenges? Be honest with yourself and adjust your "sails" so that you can enjoy the victories as your skills increase.

DIAMOND ASSIGNMENT

Reflection and Focus Items

Victories:

1.

2.

3.

4.

5.

Challenges:

1.

2.

3.

4.

5.

"THE CIRCLE OF LIFE" AND REAL ESTATE

We have come to the last chapter only to end with some thoughts that were shared in the beginning. Learn to serve buyers and sellers by providing the best customer experience available to them in the real estate industry and repeat that daily, weekly or monthly depending on your goals.

You are the "Calm and Knowledgeable Guide" leading your clients through what is often an emotionally charged experience. The mechanics of the transaction will soon be mastered and eventually will become repetitive and sometimes boring. The repetition of the process is made tolerable through the uniqueness of each home and the dynamics of the relationships involved in the sale. It is nearly impossible to become bored or unchallenged as a Realtor®.

As stated by Diane Disney, "without the wonderful people who are a part of this, it wouldn't be nearly what it is, it would be empty." We do not sell houses; we provide a service that helps people. Sometimes we get to be a part of happy exciting times. We can be transported into the emotional highs of anticipating the birth of a child as we assist the pregnant first-time homebuyer. We celebrate when that same buyer calls us years later to buy the bigger home when she gets the big promotion at work. We are the steadfast trusted advisor after the unexpected death of a parent. We are the neutral negotiator when assets have to be divided in a divorce. Honor our profession by being professional and dedicated to service at the highest level.

As a broker, I met with agents that were ready to give up just as they were about to reap the benefits of their efforts. These same agents also became some of our top producers. Frustration is a good indicator that we are doing the right thing. There is plenty of work done today that will not pay dividends for many years, sometimes decades. You are building relationships with a view to your role as a trusted real estate advisor, knowledgeable resource, and provider of superior service.

By consistently engaging in the real estate essentials, we build momentum and one day it just starts happening. Service will only materialize into closed sales when it is the right time for the buyers and sellers we serve, not on our time table.

Some agents, that have immediate results, transition out of the business because they never connect that it is always more than a transaction for the Realtors® that have long term success. A career in real estate is not for everyone, and that is a good thing. New technologies and business models are exposing the agents that don't love what they do. Only agents that build a reputation for superior service will shine when held up against the sterile, transactional experience encapsulated by some of the new models.

Travel agencies existed on every corner when I first got my real estate license. The travel industry was overtaken by technology, and yet, who of us would travel to a foreign country without the use of a guide. Our in-depth knowledge and skill will be our advantage, and our relationships will be our access to new business. Dedicate yourself to building knowledge, skill, and relationships every day!

As a trainer I have taught for many years that real estate sales are dependent on two things: Competence and confidence. These pages have been dedicated to assisting with competence. Taking action will build your confidence. Without both, success will be elusive. If you are competent without confidence, you need more practice and to take more action. If you are confident without competence, you are a jerk. Don't be a jerk! That is real estate common sense.

APPENDIX

Business Builders

✓ Goal Setting
✓ Business Planning
✓ EZ Prospecting Plan

Video instruction and printable versions of these
documents can be found on
www.RealEstateCommonSense.com

GOAL SETTING USING "NEEDLE MOVERS"

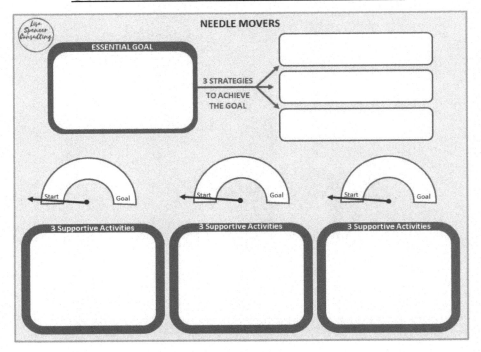

DIAMOND ASSIGNMENT

Create focus on your essential goal with the "Needle Movers" guide.

Video instruction and the "Needle Mover" template are available on www.RealEstateCommonSense.com for download.

1. Start by setting the "Essential Goal" using pages 41-45
2. Select 3 "Strategies" using pages 9-21
3. Apply numeric measuring points to your needle gauge
4. List at least 3 specific and measurable "Supportive Activities" within each of the strategy categories.

THE 10 MINUTE BUSINESS PLAN

Codes:

TL = Target Listings   AL = Actual Listings

TS = Target Sales   AS = Actual Sales

January	February	March
TL _____ AL _____	TL _____ AL _____	TL _____ AL _____
TS _____ AS _____	TS _____ AS _____	TS _____ AS _____
Income: _____	Income: _____	Income: _____
Other _____	Other _____	Other _____
+ or - _____	+ or - _____	+ or - _____

April	May	June
TL _____ AL _____	TL _____ AL _____	TL _____ AL _____
TS _____ AS _____	TS _____ AS _____	TS _____ AS _____
Income: _____	Income: _____	Income: _____
Other _____	Other _____	Other _____
+ or - _____	+ or - _____	+ or - _____

July	August	September
TL _____ AL _____	TL _____ AL _____	TL _____ AL _____
TS _____ AS _____	TS _____ AS _____	TS _____ AS _____
Income: _____	Income: _____	Income: _____
Other _____	Other _____	Other _____
+ or - _____	+ or - _____	+ or - _____

October	November	December
TL _____ AL _____	TL _____ AL _____	TL _____ AL _____
TS _____ AS _____	TS _____ AS _____	TS _____ AS _____
Income: _____	Income: _____	Income: _____
Other _____	Other _____	Other _____
+ or - _____	+ or - _____	+ or - _____

EZ PROSPECTING PLAN

Copy and past this template into your email. Send it to yourself at the end of each day thus providing a "call list" for tomorrow.

1: **Call all of the people waiting to hear from you:**

Name: _____Result: _____

Name: _____Result: _____

Name: _____Result: _____

Name: _____Result: _____

2: **Weekly call to all current buyers**

Name: _____Result: _____

Name: _____Result: _____

Name: _____Result: _____

Name: _____Result: _____

Name: _____Result: _____

3: **Weekly call to all current sellers (even if there have been no showings on their home):**

Name: _____Result: _____

Name: _____Result: _____

Name: _____Result: _____

Name: _____Result: _____

Name: _____Result: _____

4: **Contact 5 members of your sphere of influence regarding your monthly real estate topic:**

Name: _____Result: _____

Name: _____Result: _____

Name: _____Result: _____

Name: _____Result: _____

Name: _____Result: _____

5: **Ask for business and referrals!**

The Buyer Experience

✓ Home Purchase Timeline
✓ "Fair Trade" Buyer Agreement
✓ Buyer Experience Checklist

Video instruction and printable versions of these
documents can be found on
www.RealEstateCommonSense.com

HOME PURCHASE TIMELINE

Interview Realtors to determine the strongest advocate and guide to help you achieve your goals.

Connect with a mortgage lender to confirm your purchasing power!

Your REALTOR will:
- Present your offer
- Negotiate Price and Terms
- Facilitate Inspections
- Navigate Timelines

Your REALTOR is your calm and knowledgeable guide throughout the transaction.

Search for a home that meets your budget and lifestyle. Then make an offer to purchase.

Your contract will require application for a loan in a specific time frame. Locating and providing required documents is essential at this time.

The title company or attorney will often hold your escrow deposit. They will research the property to insure your purchase. The closing is usually held here.

The day of closing is a busy and exciting day of achievement . . . Celebrate!!!

3 CHOICE BUYER AGREEMENT

Thank you for the opportunity to provide you with comprehensive real estate services.

Today we will tour the following properties:

_____

_____

_____

_____

_____

No fee will be charged in advance for my services. It is customary for the seller of property to offer cooperating brokers a commission. You have a choice in Realtors® . . . Please select one of the following options:

- ○ I have an established relationship with _____ and I would like to purchase any home through him/her.

- ○ I agree that if I purchase any of the homes shown today, I will make an offer through _____

- ○ I have chosen _____as my "Exclusive Buyer Representative" and I understand that I should inform builders, other Realtors®, and sellers marketing their home on their own, that I will make offers, negotiate, and complete any purchase through _____.

Buyer: _____   Date_____

Buyer: _____   Date_____

Sales Associate: _____   Date _____

BUYER EXPERIENCE CHECKLIST (check with your broker for compliance)

Buyer "Start to Finish"

* This checklist follows the Florida FAR- BAR "AS IS" Contract. It is intended as a model only.

Initial Meeting:

- [ ] Obtain a copy of Buyer's Pre-Approval
- [ ] **Explain Agency and Signed "Transition to Transaction Broker" if necessary**
- [ ] **Signed** Buyer Disclosure Form (Transaction Fee must be disclosed if you are charging one)
- [ ] **Signed** Home Inspection "Why you should obtain one" (Required for FHA)
- [ ] Review Availability of Home Warranty   Accepted _____   Declined _____
- [ ] Offer Listing Services to Buyer Accepted _____ Declined _____
  Referred to: _____
- [ ] Provide Buyer with a Blank Sales Contract

Writing the Offer through Signed Contract:

- [ ] Review and Initial CMA
- [ ] **Delivered Lead Paint Brochure (For properties older than 1978)**
- [ ] **Signed** Lead Paint Disclosure and Delivered Lead Paint Disclosure **(Homes built prior to 1978)**
- [ ] Homeowners' Association/Community Disclosure
  Delivered _____ **Signed** _____
- [ ] Sellers Disclosure or Vacant Land Disclosure
  Delivered _____ **Signed** _____
- [ ] Provide "Buyer's Estimated Expenses" (Usually through the lender)
- [ ] **Initial Deposit:**   (Check must be delivered to Escrow Agent Immediately)
- [ ] **Escrow Verification Form Complete and turned in with file**
- [ ] Updated Buyer's Mortgage Pre-Approval *Provide Copy to Seller: _____
- [ ] **Signed Contract**
- [ ] Additional Addenda : _____
- [ ] Reviewed Contract for Signatures and Initials (all pages and addenda)
- [ ] Record Effective Date on Contract   Effective Date: _____
- [ ] Deliver Executed Contracts to all parties (Electronic OK)
  Delivered   _____
- [ ] **Submit file to office / compliance within 24 hours**

Transaction Management – (Assumes a FAR –BAR "As Is" Contract)

- [ ] **Additional Deposit:** _____ (Initial Deposit Delivered To Escrow Agent)
- [ ] Who will hold additional deposit:
  _____ (If Applicable)
- [ ] Forwarded Signed Escrow Deposit Verification to all parties
- [ ] Additional Deposit: Due: _____ Received: _____ or Confirmed
- [ ] **Provide Parties with Copy of Contact Sheet with the following:**
- [ ] Title Company Information
- [ ] Mortgage Company Information
- [ ] Appraisal Company   Scheduled: _____ Complete: _____
- [ ] Home Inspection Company Scheduled: _____ Complete: _____
- [ ] **Must Cancel By:** _____
  Repair Addendum: _____
  Date Agreed and Signed _____
  Cancellation of Contract Sent: _____
  Deposit Returned: _____

- [ ] **Mortgage Commitment:** Due: _____ Provided: _____
  (Notify All Parties if Not)

- [ ] Termite Inspection done no more than 30 days prior to closing!
  Completed : _____
- [ ] Title Work Complete   Completed : _____
- [ ] Survey Ordered by Title Company and Provided to Buyer _____
  (Contract Calls for 5 Days prior to closing)
- [ ] Confirm Buyer's Homeowner Insurance (Two Weeks Prior Especially
  Important during Hurricane Season)

Closing Preparation

- [ ] Closing Date Confirmed: Date: _____
- [ ] Confirm utilities have been disconnected by seller
- [ ] **Provide Utility Information for Buyer**
- [ ] Schedule Final Walk-Through Date: _____
- [ ] Review Closing Statement for:
  Commission _____Credits _____Transaction fee _____
  Home Warranty _____ Other: _____
- [ ] **Signed and Complete Buyer Walk-Through Acknowledgement and add office file**
- [ ] Collect Keys _____   Garage Door Openers _____
  Gate Codes/Openers _____ Security Codes _____

☐ Did Listing Agent Remove?   Lockbox _____ and Sign_____
☐ Attend Closing: Where:

_____
          When: _____
☐ Confirm the following documentation or receipts are delivered to buyer:
☐ WDO – Wood Destroying Organism Certificate Given to Buyer: _____
☐ Home Warranty: Check for _____ from: _____Buyer _____
   Seller _____To be sent by Title Company
   Confirmation Number:_____ Check
   #:_____Sent by: _____
☐ **Bring Check, Final Walk Through, and Closing Statement from Title Company add to file**
   Say "Thank You" to all parties!

Post Closing

☐ Send Thank-You notes to: Title Co. _____
☐ Other Agent: _____ Other: _____
☐ Closing Gift   Ordered: _____ Delivered: _____
☐ Order "Just Sold" Postcards
☐ Enter Customer in Database
☐ Follow Up Two Weeks After Closing
☐ *Ask for Referrals!*

Confirm your state requirements with your broker.

An editable version of this document is available on
www.RealEstateCommonSense.com for download.
Updating this checklist will assist you in developing and
maintaining systems and deadlines.

The Seller Experience

- ✓ 3 Types of Buyer
- ✓ Knowledgeable Guide
- ✓ Seller Experience Checklist

Video instruction and printable versions of these
documents can be found on
www.RealEstateCommonSense.com

3 TYPES OF BUYER

THE IDEAL BUYER

The "ideal buyer" is moving in from out of the area, and depends on the services provided by local real estate professionals.

They rely on their Realtor® for area information, guided tours, and insight into local economic growth and community development.

These buyers are relocating within a specific time frame and need a home now. They are usually willing to pay market value for a home in order to meet their time constraints. They welcome the guidance of their Realtor® as an essential part of a successful move.

THE LOCAL BUYER

A change in circumstance or the desire to buy a first home is often the motivation for the local buyer.

These "locals" know the neighborhoods, and the pace of area real estate sales. They will often wait for just the right house, and can pass on options above fair market value.

Local buyers prefer to work with their Realtor® because they need help with coordinating the sale of a previous home, help with financing options, or guidance as first time homebuyers. They often have trusted real estate professionals in their circle of friends and family.

THE INVESTOR

Investors and Institutional Buyers are looking for bargains.

If they are "flipping" the home, they must be aware of the margins for profit, and usually use a "wholesale" number rather than market value in their calculations.

The iBuyer revolution creates a convenience factor for home sellers that may be worth the reduced retention of equity, but most sellers would rather realize the highest return on their original investment.

CALM AND KNOWLEDGEABLE GUIDE

Your Knowledgeable Resource for Pricing Information

PRICE IS THE WINDOW THROUGH WHICH BUYERS SEARCH FOR A HOME!

Obtaining the best sale price for your home often depends on reaching the maximum buyer pool during the first weeks of marketing.

If a home is priced in the wrong window it will linger on the market and cause buyers to question why it hasn't sold.

Over estimating value may put obtaining the "Best Price" at risk.

Testing the market at a higher price during the critical first 30 days of marketing decreases exposure to the maximum buyer pool.

Reductions in price and length of time on the market tend to solicit lower offers from buyers.

Your Guide throughout the Transaction

80% OF THE VALUE PROVIDED BY A REALTOR OFTEN HAPPENS AFTER SECURING A BUYER!

Having a calm and knowledgeable guide that will help you navigate the process between executed contract through moving day can prove invaluable.

Realtors® are connectors in the community, skilled negotiators serving as your advocate, and the facilitator of all of the activities involved in a real estate transaction.

Coordinating the efforts of mortgage lenders, title companies, surveyors and appraisers are only the beginning of the many vendors Realtors® interact with to ensure a smooth transaction.

You deserve access to this incredible resource!

SELLER EXPERIENCE CHECKLIST

(check with your broker for compliance to state law and local protocols)

Required Forms:

☐	**Signed** Exclusive Right of Sale Listing Agreement
☐	**Signed** Homeowners' Association/Community Disclosure
☐	Sellers Property Disclosure or Vacant Land Disclosure
☐	Delivered _____ Returned _____
☐	Review Availability of Home Warranty
☐	Accepted _____ Declined _____
☐	**Signed** MLS Profile Sheet (Listing Input Sheet)
☐	**Signed** Lead Paint Disclosure and Delivered Lead Paint Brochure **(Homes built prior to 1978)**
☐	**Signed** Seller's Estimated Expenses
☐	Print-Out of County Tax Record
☐	Print-Out of MLS "Full View- Agent Synopsis"
☐	**Signed** Office Disclosures **(Transaction Fee Must Be Disclosed IF You Are Charging One)**
☐	Affiliated Business Disclosure – If Required

Listing Data:

☐	Review and Initial CMA
☐	Provide Seller a Blank Sales Contract
☐	Make a Copy of: Deed _____ Survey _____
☐	Back Title _____ Tax Roll _____
☐	Obtain Info. for: School _____ Town _____
☐	Sub-Div. _____ Utilities _____
☐	Set up office file or Electronic Submission
☐	Provide Seller with Copies of All Completed Listing Papers (Electronic Delivery OK)
☐	Send Thank You Note to Seller
☐	Offer Destination Services to Seller Accepted _____ Declined _____ Referred to: _____

Marketing:

☐ Take Interior and Exterior Photos of Property – Virtual Tour – Drone
Photo – Professional Photographer
☐ Install Yard Sign – Preferred Sign Company _____
☐ Install Lockbox #_____ Shackle Code _____
☐ Enter Listing and Lockbox into Supra for Automatic Entry Tracking
☐ Enter Listing into MLS   **MLS ID #** _____
☐ Promote Listing through Local: Broker Open House ___ Pitch Session ___
☐ Schedule Open House   Date _____
☐ Order Food/Beverage: From: _____
☐ Reviewed Feedback from Broker Open House with Seller
☐ Prepare brochure for print or online distribution
☐ Confirm and Enhance Listing on the following web sites:
  realtor.com   _____   Zillow.com _____
  Other _____   _____   _____
☐ Facebook Boosting Dates: _____   _____   _____   _____   _____
  _____   _____   _____
☐ Price Opinions from Agents: Gathered: _____   Reviewed: _____
  Shared with Seller: _____
☐ E-List Trac Pageview Reports: _____   _____   _____   _____   _____
☐ E-Mail Supra E-Key Showings: _____   _____   _____   _____   _____
☐ Monthly Marketing Report: _____ _____ _____ _____
☐ Price Improvement Requests: _____ _____ _____ _____

Enter your additional marketing strategies.

Transaction Management

	Reviewed Offer with Seller Sign - Counter — Ask for Resubmission
	Request Copy of Buyer's Mortgage Pre-Approval Received: _____
	Reviewed Contract for Signatures and Initials
	Confirm Effective Date on the contract
	HOA Disclosure: Provided: _____ Signed: _____
	Lead Paint Disclosure: Provided: _____ Signed: _____
	Seller's Disclosure to Buyer: Provided: _____ Signed: _____
	Additional Addenda: _____
	Deposit: _____ Will there be an additional Deposit?
	Who will hold the deposit: _____
	(Escrow Verification Form Req.)
	Additional Deposit: Due: _____ Received: _____ or Confirmed
	Enter following information into electronic file and database
	Title Company Information
	Mortgage Company Information
	Appraisal Company Scheduled: _____ Complete: _____
	Home Inspection Company Scheduled: _____ Complete: _____
	Repair Requests Made
	Request: _____ Complete: _____
	Request: _____ Complete: _____
	Request: _____ Complete: _____
	Request: _____ Complete: _____
	Termite Inspection done no more than 30 days prior to closing!
	Survey: Ordered: _____ Provided: _____
	Mortgage Commitment: Due: _____ Provided: _____

Closing Preparation

- [ ] Closing Date Confirmed: Date: _____
- [ ] Confirm utilities have been disconnected
- [ ] Advise Selling Agent of disconnected utilities
- [ ] Schedule Final Walk-Through Date: _____
- [ ] Review Closing Statement for:
- [ ] Commission _____ Credits _____ Transaction fee _____
- [ ] Home Warranty _____ Other: _____
- [ ] Obtain a **SIGNED** Buyer Walk-Through Inspection Acknowledgement Form
- [ ] Collect Keys _____   Garage Door Openers _____
- [ ] Gate Codes/Openers _____ Security Codes _____
- [ ] Remove Lockbox _____ and Sign_____
- [ ] Attend Closing: Where:
  _____
  When: _____

Remember to say "Thank You"

- [ ] **Bring Closing Statement, Final Walk-Through and Check back to the office or Upload Electronically**

Post Closing

- [ ] Send Thank-You notes to: Title Co. _____ Other Agent: _____
  Other: _____
- [ ] Enter Customer into Follow-Up Program
- [ ] *Ask for Referrals!*

Confirm your state requirements with your broker.

An editable version of this document is available on www.RealEstateCommonSense.com for download. Updating this checklist will assist you in developing and maintaining systems and deadlines.

VISION

Our journey began with the Walt Disney legend demonstrating the power of having a vision of where you are going, who will share your experiences, and what value you will provide. It seems only fitting that our final page is dedicated to vision.

Vision is not something that will leap out of a page in a book, but rather an expression of the motives and intentions that bubble up from your heart. It is astonishing how uncomfortable the question, "what is the vision for your business" is for agents. Whether you intend to have a career as a solo agent or own a brokerage, vision is required for long term success.

Your vision is a decision. It is an important decision that will energize you when you are frustrated, or calm you when you are frenzied. Your vision does not need to fit on a bumper sticker or include the cliché of the day. Take your time to decide what your future looks like!

Did you arrive in your future with friends and family? Then, never put a buyer or seller ahead of family. Guard the anniversaries, and special moments scheduled with them. Put your personal appointments on your calendar first. Don't miss date night, or your child's school play. Who wants to arrive in the future with a bucket full of cash and no one with whom to share it?

Now visualize an award ceremony and every buyer or seller you ever assisted is seated in the audience. You are going to give an acceptance speech for the award they have given you. Why did they nominate you? What stories will they share about their experiences with you? Become the person who will humbly raise the award and know none of it was possible without them. Their success has manifested your success.

Your vision must include the success of others in order to be realized. So, dream big, work hard and include others in the plan.